WHAT WORKS:
Instructional Strategies
for Music Education

WHAT WORKS:
Instructional Strategies
for Music Education

Edited by Margaret Merrion
Foreword by Clifford Madsen

MUSIC EDUCATORS NATIONAL CONFERENCE

Cover photograph by Linda Rutledge

ISBN# 0-940796-61-9

Foreword

The careful research necessary to investigate and document strategies for music education seems both important and difficult; important because research-based procedures should provide a great deal of help and direction for instructional processes, difficult because many perceptions associated with such research have traditionally been extremely troublesome.

A great deal has been written regarding the potential contributions of applied research for the practitioner, yet controversy still exists regarding appropriate research models, the relationship of research products to actual teaching situations, and research dissemination, to name a few. Although it may appear obvious that researched strategies would prove useful to teachers, there do not seem to be many practitioners who use or highly value such information. One can disparage such attitudes, yet it seems to me that a great deal of information can be gleaned from observing such teachers and learning from their expertise. Although they appear to go about their business in a different manner than researchers, they are also very interested in learning about anything that could help them with their most difficult tasks.

It has been my experience that those who have not had the opportunity to study and to actually do research have one of four initial reactions to a research product: (1) Why did you do that? The project is seen as ranging from naive to stupid or as investigating something thought to be extremely obvious. (2) Oh yes, I know that. I use that all the time in my teaching. (3) No, I don't think so. My experience is quite the opposite. (4) That's not the study I would have done. Why didn't you do so and so?

A strong case can be made for all of the above reactions. The first reaction might be a legitimate response to esoteric research that is primarily "basic research" and not intended to help the practitioner, or the researcher might have investigated a "common sense" proposition that, although seemingly obvious, had never previously been verified. There are many of these in research literature, for example, issues relating common notated ranges to children's *tested* vocal ranges or investigating supposed transfer effects from courses in basic theory to applied music. The second and third responses are also understandable. When a successful teacher has been using a particular technique for many years, it seems quite difficult to assume that this teacher would say, "Oh, I guess I've been wrong all these years." Similarly, it is difficult to imagine a successful teacher *needing* research justification for music practices that already seem to be very effective. The last response concerning "I think I would have done something else" is not limited to music teachers; sophisticated researchers also share this proclivity when they say, "I think you used the wrong statistic" or "your dependent variable *should* have been such and such." Again this is a justifiable response to research not seen as directly relevant or perhaps missing a major point. Additionally, when researchers present their research, they seem determined to

i

"qualify it to death" so that many listeners are never quite sure if the researcher really found anything or not. Although this is a proper research attitude, it puzzles those wanting concrete suggestions.

Another issue concerns "fixed suggestions" and problems that may arise if readers assume that this volume represents exactly what the curriculum and instructional strategies should be. A document such as this is intended to stimulate much more research; more important, it should also provide a start for questioning and discussion, for continuing critical awareness of what "ought to be" as well as "what is." Just because something works does not necessarily mean that it ought to be used or implemented. There appears to be no consensus as to what our music education curriculum or instructional strategies should be. In this context, perhaps the primary function of this document should be to ask better questions concerning curricular substance in addition to finding effective strategies. Thoughtful and careful reading and analysis seem extremely important.

The following compilation of research-based strategies represents an important advance in bringing tested procedures to the classroom teacher. Even granting the many reservations researchers have with such documents, it is both proper and commendable. I suggest that each reader study carefully more than a few entries before "lifting a few" procedures that seem to be "good ideas" or before being too critical. Thoughtful questioning and sincere attempts at genuine understanding seem necessary in order to gain an overall assessment of any suggested procedure and what value such a finding might have to an individual teacher. Members of the research community have an additional responsibility to replicate, verify, add, delete, and extend this volume.

I am delighted to provide this foreword in recommending this research synthesis to colleagues. It is important as a research product from a MENC Special Interest Research Group; it is important as a collation of researched strategies to stimulate future questions and investigations; it is most important as a documented resource for music teachers.

Clifford K. Madsen
Professor and
Senior Research Award Recipient
Florida State University

Table of Contents

9. Perception Strategies

Introduction

Both music teachers and music researchers share a keen interest in instructional strategies. Teachers continually seek ways to become more effective in their instruction. Researchers wish to identify variables of teaching effectiveness and subsequenly test hypotheses that investigate the validity of such variables. Both teachers and researchers share the pursuit of optimal learning. This report is based on that common denominator and presents effective teaching strategies that work in instructional settings.

What Works: Instructional Strategies in Music Education reflects team work. A team of Instructional Strategy (INSTRAT) Special Research Interest Group (SRIG) members examined and interpreted research literature having significant conclusions for application in music instruction. These instructional strategies help teachers determine *what* they should teach, *how* they should teach, and *when* they should teach particular content. Their report was reviewed by another team of 32 music education researchers, scholars, and teachers.

The format of the report mirrors the Department of Education's *What Works* (Washington DC: Office of Educational Research and Improvement). Each report is presented in three segments: (1) the research finding; (2) comments relative to the studies supporting the finding, including a brief discussion of applications to the classroom, rehearsal, or studio; and (3) references to the research that supports the finding.

The strategies are grouped into nine categories. The first seven categories relate to specific areas of instruction: *preschool music, elementary general music, junior high general music, secondary general music, choral music, instrumental music,* and *string music.* There is a separate category that addresses strategies for *teacher education,* and the last category of *perception* will be of interest to all readers.

The INSTRAT team made efforts to synthesize the research literature comprehensively. However, omissions may seem to occur due to lack of research or conclusive findings in particular areas. As new findings emerge, revisions will be forthcoming. What follows is a substantive summary of research-based instructional strategies—that is, "what works" in music teaching.

A collaborative project such as this could only be possible with the labors of many individuals. The following music educators made this report possible:

Contributors
Steven Brown, East Central University, Ada, Oklahoma
Richard Colwell, University of Illinois, Urbana
Hildegard Froehlich, University of North Texas, Denton
Marvin Greenberg, University of Hawaii, Honolulu
Lois Harrison, University of the Pacific, Stockton, California
Judith Jellison, University of Texas, Austin
June Jetter, University of Missouri—Kansas City

Philip McClintock, Rhode Island College, Providence
Margaret Merrion, Ball State University, Muncie, Indiana
Glenn Nierman, University of Nebraska—Lincoln
Camille Smith, University of Florida, Gainesville
Keith Thompson, Valdosta State College, Valdosta, Georgia
Marilyn Vincent, Ball State University, Muncie, Indiana

The report also received careful review from a team of music researchers, scholars, and teachers:

Reviewers

Edward P. Asmus, University of Utah, Salt Lake City
Anthony Barresi, University of Wisconsin, Madison
J. David Boyle, University of Miami, Coral Gables
Patricia Shehan Campbell, Butler University, Indianapolis
Diane DeNicola, Troy State University, Troy, Alabama
Charles Elliott, University of South Carolina, Columbia
Jere Forsythe, Ohio State University, Columbus
John Geringer, University of Texas, Austin
Edwin Gordon, Temple University, Philadelphia
Paul Haack, University of Minnesota, Minneapolis
Harriet Hair, University of Georgia, Athens
Steve Hedden, University of Arizona, Tucson
Charles Hoffer, University of Florida, Gainesville
Dennis M. Holt, University of North Florida, Jacksonville
Sherman Hong, University of Southern Mississippi, Hattiesburg
Jere Humphreys, Arizona State University, Tempe
Barry E. Kopetz, University of Minnesota, Minneapolis
Joseph A. Labuta, Wayne State University, Detroit
Dorothy McDonald, University of Iowa, Iowa City
Samuel Miller, University of Houston, Houston, Texas
Sally Monsour, Georgia State University, Atlanta
David Nelson, University of Wisconsin, Madison
Marc Peretz, Ball State University, Muncie, Indiana
Ken Phillips, University of Iowa, Iowa City
Harry E. Price, University of Alabama, Tuscaloosa
Rudolf E. Radocy, University of Kansas, Lawrence
Roger Rideout, University of Oklahoma, Norman
Donald J. Shetler, Eastman School of Music, Rochester, New York
Wendy Sims, University of Missouri—Columbia
Michael J. Wagner, Florida International University, Miami
Lizabeth Wing, University of Cincinnati, Cincinnati, Ohio
Cornelia Yarbrough, Louisiana State University, Baton Rouge

Project support

This project was made possible through the generous support of Ball State University's Office of Research and College of Fine Arts. A special thank you to my secretary, Lori Kinnett, for her excellent work in preparing the final draft.

Margaret Merrion
Associate Dean
College of Fine Arts
Ball State University
Muncie, Indiana

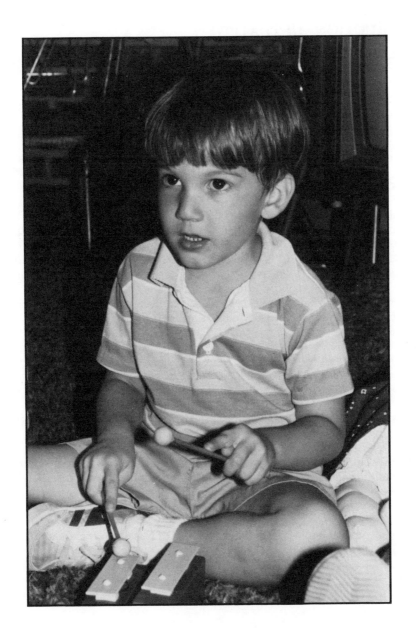

Preschool Music Strategies

Developing Musical Concepts

Research Finding: When teachers provide both positive (instances of the musical phenomenon to be observed) and negative examples (instances that do not include the musical phenomenon), new concepts can be learned effectively.

Comments: Teachers should present sufficient positive and negative examples of a musical phenomenon to ensure that the students will have grasped its critical attributes, that is, the details that have to be present for the example to be a member of the positive set. Students need to learn to ignore irrelevant characteristics, that is, those details that may be present but do not act to identify the instance as a member of the positive set.

For some concepts, the use of more negative than positive examples is more effective than the traditional use of positive examples only.

References: DeCarbo, J. (1982). The effect of same/different discrimination techniques, readiness training, pattern treatment, and sex on aural discrimination ability and singing ability of tonal patterns with kindergarten children. *Dissertation Abstracts International, 42,* 3489A. (University Microfilms No. 82-02158)

Haack, P. (1972). Use of positive and negative examples in teaching the concept of musical style. *Journal of Research in Music Education, 20,* 456–461.

Jetter, J. (1978). An instructional model for teaching identification and naming of music phenomena to preschool children. *Journal of Research in Music Education, 26,* 97–110.

Jetter, J., & Wolff, J. (1985). Effect of ratio of positive to negative instances on efficiency of musical concept learning. *Journal of Research in Music Education, 33,* 31–43.

INSTRUCTIONAL STRATEGY
Tapping and Tempo

Research Finding: The teacher's awareness of the influence of tempo upon accuracy in tapping by children should enable teacher choices leading to greater tapping accuracy by the children.

Comments: Children's synchronous tapping accuracy has been found to increase with age; certain populations are found to respond more accurately to certain tempos even though accuracy is less at extremes of fast and slow tempos. Preschool children tap more accurately at faster tempos than at slower tempos. Learning-disabled children perform better at slower speeds than at faster speeds.

Even when the tempo of the stimulus remains the same, children seem to tap imitative responses faster than the stimulus and tend to accelerate subsequent responses; they are able to respond more accurately when tapping than when doing more complex, but traditional, forms of response such as marching.

Teachers who sequence tapping experiences with regard for appropriate tempos will help students achieve greater accuracy of response in both synchronous and imitative activities.

References: Atterbury, B. (1983). A comparison of rhythm pattern perception and performance in normal and learning-disabled readers, age seven and eight. *Journal of Research in Music Education, 31,* 259–270.

Brunt, D., Magill, R., & Eason, R. (1983). Distinctions in variability of motor output between learning disabled and normal children. *Perceptual and Motor Skills, 57,* 731–734.

Cox, M. (1977). A descriptive analysis of the response to beat, meter, and rhythm pattern by children in grades one to six. *Dissertation Abstracts International, 38,* 3353A. (University Microfilms No. 77-17818)

Gilbert, J. (1983). A comparison of the motor music skills of nonhandicapped and learning-disabled children. *Journal of Research in Music Education, 31,* 147–155.

Grieshaber, K. (1987). Children's rhythmic tapping: A critical review of research. *Bulletin of the Council for Research in Music Education, 90,* 73–81.

Jersild, A., & Bienstock, S. (1935). *A study of the development of rhythm in young children.* New York: Bureau of Publications, Teachers College, Columbia University.

Osbum, G. (1981). *Measuring children's rhythmic skills using two rhythmic pattern imitation tests.* Unpublished master's thesis, University of Washington, Seattle.

Petzold, R. (1963). The development of auditory perception of musical sounds by children in the first six grades. *Journal of Research in Music Education, 11,* 21–43.

Rainbow, E. (1981). A final report on a three-year investigation of the rhythmic abilities of pre-school aged children. *Bulletin of the Council for Research in Music Education, 66–67,* 69–73.

Smoll, F. (1975). Preferred tempo of motor performance: Individual differences in within-individual variability. *Journal of Motor Behavior, 7,* 259–263.

Williams, H., Sievers, C., & Hattwick, M. (1933). The measure of musical development. *University of Iowa Studies in Child Welfare, 7*(1), 1–191.

Using Movement

Research Finding: **Children's movements to music are diverse but are greatly influenced by observation of peers. Clapping and marching to the beat are very difficult skills.**

Comments: Children are highly imitative in their movements to music. Expressive movement is significantly influenced by the tendency of children to imitate their peers.

Clapping or marching may be questionable practices to assess young children's responses to beat. Careful observation of different types of movements children demonstrate can assist teachers in choosing appropriate movement activities.

References: Flohr, J., & Brown, J. (1979). The influence of peer imitation on expressive movement to music. *Journal of Research in Music Education, 27,* 143–148.

Rainbow, E. (1977). A longitudinal report on a three year investigation of the rhythmic abilities of preschool aged children. *Bulletin of the Council for Research in Music Education, 66–67,* 69–73.

Schleuter, S., & Schleuter, L. (1985). The relationship of grade level and sex differences to certain rhythmic responses of primary grade children. *Journal of Research in Music Education, 33,* 23–29.

INSTRUCTIONAL STRATEGY
Selecting Music for Listening

Research Finding: **Selecting suitable music to play for children to develop appreciative listening skills is important.**

Comments: Music selected for listening should be high-quality examples from a variety of music styles and historical periods. It should also represent literature with obvious or prominent musical characteristics.

"Liking" a piece of music is the result of the subjective complexity of the listening, the objective characteristics of the piece, and the listener's musical experience and sophistication.

Select music and plan for cognitive, kinesthetic, and affective activities. Teachers should take into account both the complexity of the music and the experience, cognitive styles, and conceptual development of listeners. Optimal results may be obtained when the teacher employs music examples that emphasize certain attributes for listeners of a specific age.

References: Gardner, H. (1973). Children's sensitivity to musical styles. *Merrill Palmer Quarterly, 19*, 67–77.

Hargreaves, D. (1984). The effects of repetition on liking for music. *Journal of Research in Music Education, 32*, 35–47.

Hedden, S. (1981). Music listening skills and music listening preferences. *Bulletin of the Council for Research in Music Education, 65*, 16–26.

Lenz, S. (1978). A case study of the musical abilities of three-and four-year old children. *Dissertation Abstracts International, 39*, 2809A. (University Microfilms No. 78-20990)

Lott, V. (1978). A study of musical achievement of culturally disadvantaged preschool children based on the Music for Preschool curriculum of Marvin Greenberg. *Dissertation Abstracts International, 39*, 1183A. (University Microfilms No. 78-15630)

Parker, J. (1972). Discriminative listening as a basis for problem solving among four-year olds. *Dissertation Abstracts International, 33*, 4460. (University Microfilms No. 73-04208)

Trammel, P. (1978). An investigation of the effectiveness of repetition and guided listening in developing enjoyable music listening experiences for second grade students. *Dissertation Abstracts International, 38*, 5323A. (University Microfilms No. 78-01781)

INSTRUCTIONAL STRATEGY

Controlling Duration of Listening Time

Research Finding: The length of music chosen for a listening experience must be appropriate to the children's attention span. It has been suggested that preschool children can maintain attention to musical selections that do not exceed 2 minutes in length.

Comments: The older the children are, the lengthier the music excerpts that can be played for them (provided they know how to listen and what to listen for). Music listening attention span increases uniformly and in a directional, predictable manner with advancement in grade level. In one researcher's opinion, this development is not linear.

References: Dressler, D. (1970). A music record library for preschool children. *Dissertation Abstracts International, 32*, 1548A. (University Microfilms No. 71-024143)

Flohr, J. (1980). Musical improvisation behavior of young Flohr children. *Dissertation Abstracts International, 40*, 5355A. (University Microfilms No. 80-09033)

Greer, R., Dorow, L., & Randall, A. (1974). Music listening preferences of elementary school children. *Journal of Research in Music Education, 22*, 284–291.

Trammel, P. (1978). An investigation of the effectiveness of repetition and guided listening in developing enjoyable music listening experiences for second grade students. *Dissertation Abstracts International, 38*, 5323A. (University Microfilms No. 78-01781)

INSTRUCTIONAL STRATEGY
Repeating Listening Selections

Research Finding: **Repeated exposure to particular music—either a specific piece or a particular style—will increase liking for that music.**

Comments: Exposure and repetition, along with a positive classroom environment, and experience emphasizing social reinforcement, can affect the musical preferences of children. A program of analytic listening and repetition results in greater preference changes than a program of repeated listening.

Preschool children are musically sensitive to various types of music and can discriminate among different music styles. Since musical taste develops at a very early stage, more emphasis is needed on the development of home-based and school-based music listening programs for the very young.

"Liking" scores for a given piece increase between the initial hearing and the sixth to eighth hearing, but decline afterward. Excessive exposure will result, then, in decreased liking. There is a relationship among repeated exposure, complexity of music, sophistication of the listener, and repeated listening. An optimal strategy may be to plan for six to eight hearings of a piece over one semester.

References: Bradley, I. (1971). Repetition as a factor in the development of music preferences. *Journal of Research in Music Education, 19,* 295–298.

Edmonston, W. (1969). Familiarity and musical training in the esthetic evaluation of music. *Journal of Social Psychology, 79,* 109–111.

Getz, R. (1966). The influence of familiarity through repetition in determining music preference. *Journal of Research in Music Education, 14,* 178–192.

Hargreaves, D. (1984). The effects of repetition on liking for music. *Journal of Research in Music Education, 32,* 35–47.

Heingartner, A., & Hall, J. (1974). Affective consequences in adults and children of repeated exposure to auditory stimuli. *Journal of Personality and Social Psychology, 29,* 719–723.

Heyduk, R. (1975). Rated preference for musical compositions as it relates to complexity and exposure frequency. *Perception & Psychophysics, 17,* 84–90.

Hoover, P. (1974). A synthesis of the findings of research related to the process of listening to music, the status of the research and implications for music education. *Dissertation Abstracts International, 35,* 5446A. (University Microfilms No. 75-03883)

Mull, H. (1957). The effect of repetition upon the enjoyment of modern music. *Journal of Psychology, 43,* 155–164.

Peery, J., & Peery, I. (1986). Effects of exposure to classical music on the musical preferences of preschool children. *Journal of Research in Music Education, 34,* 24–33.

Rogers, V. (1957). Children's musical preferences as related to grade level and other factors. *Elementary School Journal, 57,* 433–435.

Schuckert, R., & McDonald, R. (1968). An attempt to modify the musical preferences of preschool children. *Journal of Research in Music Education, 16,* 39–44.

Sluckin, W., Hargreaves, D., & Coleman, A. (1982). Some experimental studies of familiarity and liking. *Bulletin of the British Psychological Society, 355,* 189–194.

INSTRUCTIONAL STRATEGY
Participating Actively During Listening Lessons

Research Finding: Activities requiring active participation, such as singing themes, playing instruments to accompany the music, following written scores, and movement to the music are associated with higher levels of attention than are more passive types of activities such as discussion or the use of listening to tapes with written or verbal explanations.

Comments: For children below ages 6 or 7, nonverbal techniques are the best way to promote listening response. For example, the use of specific, simple body movements increases listening skills in early childhood music. At all times, teachers should direct children to attend to a specific aspect of the music to which they can respond.

References: Abel-Struth, S. (1981). Frankfurt studies on musical audiation of five to seven year old children. *Bulletin of the Council for Research in Music Education, 66–67,* 1–7.

Forsythe, J. (1977). Elementary student attending behavior as a function of classroom activities. *Journal of Research in Music Education, 25,* 228–239.

Madsen, C., & Alley, J. (1979). The effect of reinforcement on attentiveness: A comparison of behaviorally trained music therapists and other professionals with implications for competency-based academic preparation. *Journal of Music Therapy, 16,* 70–82.

Madsen, C., & Madsen, C. (1972). Selection of music listening or candy as a function of contingent versus non-contingent reinforcement and scale singing. *Journal of Music Therapy, 9,* 190–198.

Madsen, C., Wolfe, D., & Madsen, C. (1969). The effect of reinforcement and directional scalar methodology on intonation improvement. *Bulletin of the Council for Research in Music Education, 18,* 22–33.

Peery, J., & Peery, I. (1986). Effects of exposure to classical music on the musical preferences of preschool children. *Journal of Research in Music Education, 34,* 24–33.

Simon, G. (1986). Early childhood musical development: A survey of selected research. *Bulletin of the Council for Research in Music Education, 86,* 36–52.

Sims, W. (1986). The effect of high versus low teacher affect versus active student activity during music listening on preschool children's attention, piece preference, time spent listening, and piece recognition. *Journal of Research in Music Education, 34,* 173–191.

Stone, M. (1983). Some antecedents of music appreciation. *Psychology of Music, 11*(1), 26–31.

Van Zee, N. (1975). Verbal-descriptive and performance responses of kindergarten children to selected musical stimuli and terminology. *Dissertation Abstracts International, 35,* 4604A. (University Microfilms No. 75-1280)

INSTRUCTIONAL STRATEGY
Affecting Students' Musical Preferences

Research Finding:	**Factors such as teacher verbal approval, nonverbal affective approval, peer approval, and modeling influence listening preferences of children more than does analytical study.**

A high degree of teacher affect during listening experiences produces more attentiveness on the part of preschoolers. "High teacher affect" is defined as frequent eye contact and the use of facial expressions that indicate excitement, happiness, and enthusiasm. "Low teacher affect" is defined as little or no eye contact (maintaining a bored facial expression) during listening.

Comments: Approval is better than no approval in influencing listening preferences of children. High teacher approval is one of the most effective instructional variables for determining music selection behavior. Music taught with high approval will result in more time spent listening.

The use of teacher eye contact and magnitude of facial expression affects listening responses in children. Provided these nonverbal expressions do not distract, teacher eye contact and facial expression indicating excitement, happiness, and enthusiasm have a positive impact.

Teachers of preschool listening should observe students' level of attentiveness to the music. The teachers can adjust their own level of excitement in response to the music to modify students' responses. A large number of inappropriate behaviors may occur while listening to music due to teachers' misuse of affect. Too much affect, for instance, may cause inappropriate responses.

Teachers may control pupil behavior by monitoring the level of excitement displayed during listening. Preservice teachers should practice observing student responses and altering their own behavior during listening.

References: Baker, D. (1980). The effect of appropriate and inappropriate in-class song performance models on performance preference of third-and fourth-grade students. *Journal of Research in Music Education, 28,* 3–17.

Dorow, L. (1977). The effect of teacher approval/disapproval ratios on student music selection and concert attentiveness. *Journal of Research in Music Education, 25,* 32–40.

Greer, R., Dorow, L., & Hanser, S. (1973). Music discrimination training and the music selection behavior of nursery and primary level children. *Bulletin of the Council for Research in Music Education, 22,* 284–291.

Greer, R., Dorow, L., Wachhaus, G., & White, E. (1973). Adult approval and students' music selection behavior. *Journal of Research in Music Education, 21,* 345–354.

Hedden, S. (1981). Development of music listening skills. *Bulletin of the Council for Research in Music Education, 64,* 12–22.

Madsen, C., & Forsythe, J. (1973). Effect of contingent music listening on increases of mathematical responses. *Journal of Research in Music Education, 21,* 176–181.

Madsen, C., & Madsen, C. (1972). Selection of music listening or candy as a function of contingent versus non-contingent reinforcement and scale singing. *Journal of Music Therapy, 9,* 190–198.

Pantle, J. (1977). The effect of teacher approval of music on selection and musical verbal preference. *Dissertation Abstracts International, 38,* 4010A. (University Microfilms No. 77-28002)

Shehan, P. (1984). The effect of instruction method on preference, achievement and attentiveness for Indonesian gamelan music. *Psychology of Music, 12,* no. 1, 34–42.

Sims, W. (1986). The effect of high versus low teacher affect versus active student activity during music listening on preschool children's attention, piece preference, time spent listening, and piece recognition. *Journal of Research in Music Education, 34,* 173–191.

Using Vocabulary in Listening Lessons

Research Finding: **Verbal analysis of music is important to the listening task. The ability to describe musical events in a recorded work appears to increase through the study of music terminology and its application to musical excerpts.**

Comments: As isolated activities, neither vocabulary study nor repeated listening and description of music seems to produce increased verbal attention to elements of music. The study of vocabulary with subsequent description of music excerpts may promote the use of music vocabulary to a greater degree than would isolated vocabulary study or description of music.

Young children "hear" in music more than they are able to verbalize. Music vocabulary study may be beneficial in increasing technical descriptions of changes in music. These gains are even more substantial when students are taught to apply vocabulary words to music during the learning process. Consistently labeled sounds are better recognized than are inconsistently labeled sounds.

An academic task such as answering questions or verbalizing responses may actually cause students to become off-task to the musical experience.

References: Bartlett, J. (1977). Remembering environmental sounds: The role of verbalization at input. *Memory and Cognition, 5,* 404–414.

Bower, G., & Holyoak, K. (1973). Encoding and recognition memory for naturalistic sounds. *Journal of Experimental Psychology, 101,* 360–366.

Flowers, P. (1983). The effect of instruction in vocabulary and listening on nonmusicians' descriptions of changes in music. *Journal of Research in Music Education, 31,* 179–189.

Flowers, P. (1987). The effect of written descriptions on memory of fifth graders and undergraduates for orchestral excerpts. In C. Madsen & C. Prickett (Eds.), *Applications of research in music behavior* (pp. 32–42). Tuscaloosa: University Press of Alabama.

Flowers, P. (1988). The effects of teaching and learning experiences, tempo, and mode on undergraduates' and children's symphonic music preferences. *Journal of Research in Music Education, 36,* 19–34.

Geringer, J., & Nelson, J. (1980). Effects of guided listening on music achievement and preference of fourth graders. *Perceptual and Motor Skills, 51,* 1282.

Hair, H. (1981). Verbal identification of music concepts. *Journal of Research in Music Education, 29,* 11–21.

Jetter, J. (1978). An instructional model for teaching identification and naming of music phenomena to preschool children. *Journal of Research in Music Education, 26,* 97–110.

Laurence, D. (1979). Role of verbal representations in testing recognition of naturalistic sounds. *Perceptual and Motor Skills, 48,* 443–446.

Mueller, K. (1956). Studies in music appreciation. *Journal of Research in Music Education, 4,* 3–25.

Reimer, B. (1967). *Development and trial in a junior and senior high school of a two-year curriculum in general music.* Cleveland: Case Western Reserve University. (ERIC Document Reproduction Service No. ED 017 562)

Van Zee, N. (1976). Response of kindergarten children to musical stimuli and terminology. *Journal of Research in Music Education, 24,* 14–21.

Young, L. (1982). An investigation of young children's music concept development using non-verbal and manipulative techniques. *Dissertation Abstracts International, 43,* 1345A. (University Microfilms No. 82–22205)

2

Elementary General
Music Strategies

INSTRUCTIONAL STRATEGY
Improving Children's Singing

**Research
Finding:**

Training improves children's vocal performance in specific ways. Improvement is directly related to the amount of training. Furthermore, children are more likely to sing songs with greater accuracy when teachers demonstrate a good vocal model. Children's voices as models are more accurately matched than are adult female and male voices, although the relationship between vocal pitch-matching and pitch-discrimination abilities of young children is not clear.

Comments:

Teachers who want to increase their students' vocal range, capacity for intensity, and pitch accuracy should consider adding breathing exercises to singing activities. Improvements in breath control capacity, vocal range, vocal intensity, and pitch accuracy for primary- and intermediate-level students can be made through classroom instruction.

Teachers must be careful to model songs in class exactly as they are to be performed by children, providing the best vocal quality possible for children to emulate. Male teachers are advised to use falsetto in classes with uncertain singers. Because vocal instruction takes place in group settings, the use of falsetto may have mixed results.

References:

Baker, D. (1980). The effect of appropriate and inappropriate in-class song performance models in performance preference of third- and fourth-grade students. *Journal of Research in Music Education, 28,* 3–17.

Geringer, J. (1983). The relationship of pitch-matching and pitch-discrimination abilities of preschool and fourth-grade students. *Journal of Research in Music Education, 31,* 93–99.

Gould, A. (1968). *Developing specialized programs for singing in the elementary school* (Final Report). Washington, DC: Research in Education. (ERIC Document Reproduction Service ED 02554024 TE 499967)

Green, G. (1987). The effect of vocal modeling on pitch-matching of children in grades one through six. *Dissertation Abstracts International, 48,* 1410A. (University Microfilms No. 87-19865)

Phillips, K. (1985). The effects of group breath-control training on the singing ability of elementary students. *Journal of Research in Music Education, 33,* 179–191.

Ramsey, S. (1982). The effects of age, singing ability, and instrumental experiences on preschool children's melodic perception. *Journal of Research in Music Education, 31,* 133–145.

Sims, W., Moore, R., & Kuhn, T. (1982). Effects of female and male vocal stimuli, tonal pattern length, and age on vocal pitch-matching abilities of young children from England and the United States. *Psychology of Music, 10,* 104–108.

Small, A., & McCachern, F. (1983). The effect of male and female vocal modeling on pitch-matching accuracy of first-grade children. *Journal of Research in Music Education, 31,* 227–233.

Wolf, J. (1984). *An investigation of natural male voice and falsetto male voice on fourth grade children's ability to find pitch.* Unpublished master's thesis, University of Missouri–Kansas City.

INSTRUCTIONAL STRATEGY
Developing the Child Voice

Research Finding: There is a developmental continuum of singing ability that is characterized by five stages: (1) song words appear to be the center of interest with little regard for pitch, (2) sung pitch is produced with variation in accuracy, (3) more individual pitches are matched correctly, (4) pitches are fine tuned, and (5) no major pitch or melodic errors are made.

Comments: Teachers can use their knowledge of the developmental continuum to understand and help the child voice. They should exercise care in selecting songs with appropriate ranges, help children develop their head voices, and eventually ease them through their voice changes.

Current music textbooks for children incorporate few materials dealing with vocal development, especially for older children who should be instructed in basic vocal anatomy, proper posture, use and extension of the singing voice, and interpretation of song literature.

References: Goetze, M. (1985). Factors affecting accuracy in children's singing. *Dissertation Abstracts International, 46,* 2955A. (University Microfilms No. 85-28488)

Kavanaugh, J. (1983). The development of vocal concepts in children: The methodologies recommended in designated elementary music series. *Dissertation Abstracts International, 43,* 2270A. (University Microfilms No. 82-23050)

Miller, S. (1985). Upper grade vocal music: How as well as what. *Update: The Applications of Research in Music Education, 4*(1), 6–9.

Saunders, T. (1984). The relationship between young children's ability to recognize their own voice and to sing tonal patterns and to chant rhythm patterns. *Dissertation Abstracts International, 46,* 642. (University Microfilms No. 85-09391)

Wassum, S. (1979). Elementary school children's vocal range. *Journal of Research in Music Education, 27,* 214–226.

Welch, G. (1986). A developmental view of children's singing. *British Journal of Music Education, 3,* 295–303.

Using Keyboards to Increase Musical Learning

Research Finding: When teachers have children use keyboards in general music classes, the children learn more about music. Behavioral techniques and contracts have been used effectively in applied keyboard settings and may be transferred to classroom settings.

Comments: The range of keyboard instruction varies from a single keyboard primarily used by the teacher to multiple keyboards used by the children. They are used in special keyboard classes and as part of general music classes beginning with grade three. The effect of keyboard instruction is dependent upon the goals set up by the teacher and the amount of time relegated to it, but use of the keyboard in general music classes increases the children's musical knowledge in more areas than it does not. Students also seem to enjoy music class more.

An adequate number of keyboards for music classes is costly; however, prices of individual keyboards continue to decline. Beneficial effects of keyboards for general music instruction justify the expenditure.

References: Bodecker, L. (1969). Teaching music through keyboard experiences to third grade children in selected impoverished elementary schools. *Dissertation Abstracts International, 29,* 2734A. (University Microfilms No. 69-2829)

Curt, M. (1971). The use of electronic pianos to facilitate learning in seventh grade general music classes. *Dissertation Abstracts International, 32,* 997–998A. (University Microfilms No. 71-13295)

Finnell, A. (1974). The effect of keyboard experience on music achievement. *Dissertation Abstracts International, 34,* 4821A. (University Microfilms No. 74-2122)

Kostka, M. (1984). An investigation of reinforcements, time use, and student attentiveness in piano lessons. *Journal of Research in Music Education, 32,* 113–122.

Martinez, H. (1976). The development and investigation of a piano curriculum for improving music reading skills in a general music class. *Dissertation Abstracts International, 36,* 4841A. (University Microfilms No. LC 76-2671)

Wig, J., & Boyle, J. (1982). The effect of keyboard learning experiences on middle school general music students' music achievement and attitudes. *Journal of Research in Music Education, 30,* 163–172.

Wolfe, D. (1987). The use of behavioral contracts in music instruction. In C. Madsen & C. Prickett (Eds.), *Applications of research in music behavior* (pp. 43–50). Tuscaloosa: University of Alabama Press.

INSTRUCTIONAL STRATEGY
Using Classroom Musical Instruments

Research Finding: **When teachers have children use classroom instruments in general music, the children like the musical activities better and perform better.**

Comments: Classroom musical instruments include pitched and nonpitched percussion instruments, recorders, and Autoharps. Although sometimes these instruments are part of the general music class with a focus upon learning the instruments for their own sake, more often they are used to give the children musical experiences related to concept development and aesthetic involvement. Inclusion of these instruments is motivational and seems to help the children focus on the musical experience of which they are a part.

Students comment positively upon their desire to play instruments as well as showing approval with their behaviors. Successful teachers pay attention to students' preferences and include musical instruments in lessons as strong motivators.

References: Broquist, O. (1961). A survey of the attitudes of 2,594 Wisconsin elementary school pupils toward their learning experiences in music. *Dissertation Abstracts International, 22,* 1917. (University Microfilms No. 61-05897)

Geringer, J. (1977). An assessment of children's musical instrument preference. *Journal of Music Therapy, 14,* 172–179.

Nolin, W. (1973). Attitudinal growth patterns toward elementary school music experiences. *Journal of Research in Music Education, 21,* 123–134.

Pogonowski, L. (1985). Attitude assessment of upper elementary students in a process-oriented music curriculum. *Journal of Research in Music Education, 33,* 247–257.

Siemens, M. (1969). A comparison of Orff and traditional instructional methods in music. *Journal of Research in Music Education, 17,* 272–285.

Vander Ark, S., Nolin, W., & Newman, I. (1980). The relationships between musical attitudes, self-esteem, social status, and grade level of elementary children. *Bulletin of the Council for Research in Music Education, 62,* 31–41.

Listening to Music: A Developmental Process

Research Finding: **Listening is a major activity in elementary general music. There appears to be a developmental progression of listening skills. Furthermore, listening occurs on a "single track" for students under the ages of 10–12.**

Comments: Young listeners (ages 3–5) are able to identify qualities of timbre and loudness. Somewhat older listeners may recognize qualities of rhythm and pitch. Simultaneous sound events, such as harmony, are not accessible to students younger than 10–12 years of age.

Depending on the age level of the child, the process of listening to music can vary widely. Young children clearly do not hear music in the same way as do older students and adults. Listening lessons should be planned so that attention is focused on age-appropriate aspects of music.

Based on the assumption that students should develop listening skills not only while listening to recorded performance of others but also when listening to their own performance, an instrument was designed to systematically collect data on time use in elementary classrooms. In most classrooms listening is an important part of all learning activities, but students are not frequently reminded to listen.

References: Andrews, F., & Deihl, N. (1967). *Development of a technique for identifying elementary school children's musical concepts* (Cooperative Research Project 5-0233). University Park: The Pennsylvania State University.

Baldridge, W. (1984). A systematic investigation of listening activities in the elementary general music classroom. *Journal of Research in Music Education, 32,* 79–93.

Hufstader, R. (1977). An investigation of a learning sequence of music listening skills. *Journal of Research in Music Education, 25,* 184–196.

Serafine, M. (1988). *Music as cognition: The development of thought in sound.* New York: Columbia University Press.

INSTRUCTIONAL STRATEGY

Developing Listening Skills Through Programmed Instruction

Research Finding: **Some forms of programmed instruction can effectively develop listening skills.**

Comments: A number of researchers have attempted to design forms of self-instructional packages to develop listening skills. These packages have included a variety of programmed techniques including audio-visual materials and peer tutoring. Most programs were found to be as effective as traditional forms of instruction. Since the programs themselves vary widely in content and quality and the populations for whom they have been developed have been diversified, generalizations can be made only with caution.

References: Fritz, R. (1979). The development and evaluation of individual learning units in basic listening skills for prospective elementary classroom teachers. *Dissertation Abstracts International, 40,* 3614A. (University Microfilms No. 80-01732)

Harrison, L. (1974). The development and evaluation of supplementary programmed materials for teaching meter and major-minor discrimination to elementary school children. *Dissertation Abstracts International, 35,* 1144A. (University Microfilms No. 74-18718)

Jumpeter, J. (1985). Personalized system of instruction versus the lecture-demonstration methods in a specific area of a college music appreciation course. *Journal of Research in Music Education, 33,* 113–122.

Rives, J. (1970). A comparative study of traditional and programmed methods for developing music listening skills in fifth grade. *Journal of Research in Music Education, 18,* 126–133.

Tatarunis, A. (1975). *The effect of two teaching methods utilizing popular music on the ability of 7th grade students to perceive aurally and identify musical concepts.* Unpublished doctoral dissertation, Boston University, School of Education, Boston.

Zumbrunn, K. (1972). A guided listening program in twentieth century art music for junior high school students. *Journal of Research in Music Education, 20,* 370–378.

INSTRUCTIONAL STRATEGY
Motivating Listeners to Listen Attentively

Research Finding: **The development of attentive listening skills is a prerequisite or initial event of any type of learning, including listening to music. The first task in presenting a listening lesson is to motivate the listener to attend to the music.**

Comments: Attention is an active process of selecting the stimulus upon which to focus. Those aspects of the music that listeners notice will shape their musical responses. Early development of attentive listening habits and skills is basic to continued music learning and attention. The listeners must agree to attend to the stimulus. The teacher may use discussion, movement, imagery, instruments, charts, and other methods designed to get listeners to attend to the music.

References: Baldridge, W. (1984). A systematic investigation of listening activities in the elementary general music classroom. *Journal of Research in Music Education, 32,* 79–93.

Forsythe, J. (1977). Elementary student attending behavior as a function of classroom activities. *Journal of Research in Music Education, 25,* 228–239.

Gagne, R. (1977). *The conditions of learning.* New York: Holt, Rinehart and Winston.

LeBlanc, A. (1982). An interactive theory of music preference. *Journal of Music Therapy, 19,* 28–45.

INSTRUCTIONAL STRATEGY
Forming Musical Preferences

Research Finding: Elementary school students' preferences in music decline in the liking of art music as they get older. Popular music becomes the main choice between third and fourth grades with the abandonment of other style choices generally occurring at the same time.

Comments: Students and teachers are not unanimous in defining popular music. Although easy listening/popular music is the preference of fifth graders, dixieland, ragtime, band march music, country and western/bluegrass, and electronic music are statistically equal to rock in preference choice. Opera and punk rock music are generally not well liked. Fifth and sixth graders consistently prefer faster tempos, and prefer instrumental to vocal music. Rhythmic emphasis and an easily recognizable melody are important in student choice.

A critical period in music preference development appears to occur around fourth grade. Teachers who are concerned about influencing student choice of music have found that preference may be affected by repeated hearings, selections with certain student-approved traits (fast tempo, certain moods), social context, and positive reinforcement during presentation. Teacher and disc jockey approval may increase classical music preference.

References: Alpert, J. (1980). The effect of disc jockey, peer, and music teacher approval on music selection and preference. *Dissertation Abstracts International, 40,* 5641A. (University Microfilms No. 80-09822)

Deihl, E., Schneider, M., & Petress, K. (1983). Dimensions of music preference: A factor analysis study. *Popular Music and Society, 9*(3), 41–50.

Greer, R., Dorow, L., & Harrison, L. (1975). Aural discrimination instruction and the preference of sixth-graders for music listening, story listening, and candy. In C. Madsen, R. Greer, & C. Madsen, Jr. (Eds.), *Research in music behavior: Modifying music behavior in the classroom* (pp. 97–108). New York: Teachers College Press.

Hedden, S. (1981). Music listening skills and music listening preferences. *Bulletin of the Council for Research in Music Education, 65,* 16–26.

LeBlanc, A. (1979). Generic style music preferences of fifth-grade students. *Journal of Research in Music Education, 27,* 255–270.

LeBlanc, A., Colman, J., McCrary, J., Sherrill, C., & Malin, S. (1988). Tempo preferences of different age music listeners. *Journal of Research in Music Education, 36,* 156–168.

LeBlanc, A., & Cote, R. (1983). Effects of tempo and performing medium on children's music preference. *Journal of Research in Music Education, 31,* 57–66.

May, W. (1985). Musical style preferences and aural discrimination skills of primary grade school children. *Journal of Research in Music Education, 33,* 7–22.

Shehan, P. (1984). The effect of instruction method on preference, achievement and attentiveness for Indonesian gamelan music. *Psychology of Music, 12,* no. 1, 34–42.

Shehan, P. (1985). Transfer of preference from taught to untaught pieces of non-Western music genres. *Journal of Research in Music Education, 33,* 149–158.

Shehan, P. (1986). Towards tolerance and taste: Preferences for world music. *British Journal of Music Education, 3,* 153–163.

Sims, W. (1987). Effect of tempo on music preference of preschool through fourth grade children. In C. Madsen & C. Prickett (Eds.), *Applications of research in music behavior* (pp. 15–25). Tuscaloosa: University of Alabama Press.

Wapnick, J. (1976). A review of research on attitude and preference. *Bulletin of the Council for Research in Music Education, 48,* 1–20.

Increasing Preference Through Repetition in Listening

Research Finding: **Several opportunities to listen to the same musical selection, with attention guided to specific aspects of the music, tend to increase students' enjoyment in listening to music.**

Comments: Students appear to profit most from 3 or 4 in-depth listening experiences with a given composition or excerpt. Saturation may occur if experiences are repeated too frequently. Negative effects on enjoyment also may occur with too many repetitions.

References: Getz, R. (1966). The influence of familiarity through repetition in determining music preference. *Journal of Research in Music Education, 14,* 178–192.

Hargreaves, D. (1984). The effects of repetition on liking for music. *Journal of Research in Music Education, 32,* 35–47.

Trammell, P. (1977). An investigation of the effectiveness of repetition and guided listening in developing enjoyable music listening experiences for second grade students. *Dissertation Abstracts International, 38,* 5323A. (University Microfilms No. 78-01781)

Walker, E. (1981). Hedgehog theory and music education. In *Documentary Report of the Ann Arbor Symposium* (pp. 317–328). Reston, VA: Music Educators National Conference.

Modifying Listening Instruction

**Research
Finding:** **Teachers can develop vocabulary effectively through selective choice of
materials and appropriate teaching behaviors.**

Comments: Teaching for vocabulary development in schools where students have been deprived of
listening experiences may require different instructional materials and different
teacher behaviors. For example, teachers should choose materials for use in inner-city
classes that encourage students to talk about music. The needs and interests of the
students must be taken into consideration. (This may preclude using the same music
book at the same grade level for all students in a school district.)

Additionally, teachers should employ a teaching style that will most actively involve
inner-city students in the listening task.

References: McDonald, D. (1974). Environment—A factor in conceptual listening skills of elementary school children. *Journal of Research in Music Education, 22,* 205–214.

Madsen, C. (1982). The effect of contingent teacher approval and withholding music
performance on improving attentiveness. *Psychology of Music, 10,* 76–81.

INSTRUCTIONAL STRATEGY
Setting Mutual Instructional Objectives

Research Finding: Instructional objectives stated by music teachers may be at variance with objectives valued by elementary children.

Comments: A mismatch of teacher and student preferred objectives may result in negative attitudes by the students with an accompanying lack of interest in learning. It is important that music teachers gain information about students' objectives. It is often possible that the music teacher can meet student objectives while at the same time attaining educational objectives of importance to the teacher.

Teachers need to be aware of the negative effects of establishing a hierarchy of objectives based on a student's intellectual "label." It is important that teachers individualize instruction but maintain a single curriculum that is valued for all children.

Students seem to value complete musical performances using instruments and having as much freedom of expression as possible. Some research also indicates this is more effective than the piecemeal approach currently advocated by some educators. If the assumption is accurate that children learn more readily using activities they prefer, identification of student preferences and application of them to educational objectives developed by the teacher will increase student learning and positive attitudes toward music learning.

References: Burton, W. (1962). *The guidance of learning activities* (3rd ed.). New York: Appleton-Century-Crofts.

Franklin, J., & Nicholson, E. (1978). Relationship between teacher viewpoints towards a culturally oriented music program and black pupils' achievement and viewpoints towards the program. *Education, 98,* 307–310.

Jellison, J., & Wolfe, D. (1987). Educators' ratings of selected objectives for severely handicapped or gifted students in the classroom. *Contributions to Music Education, 14,* 36–41.

Murphy, M., & Brown, T. (1986). A comparison of preferences for instructional objectives between teachers and students. *Journal of Research in Music Education, 34,* 134–139.

Wessler, R. (1976). An assessment of achievement and attitudes toward music among fourth, fifth and sixth grade students in Corazal, Puerto Rico. *Dissertation Abstracts International, 37,* 6336A–6337A. (University Microfilms No. 77-9239)

INSTRUCTIONAL STRATEGY
Using Computer-Assisted Instruction: Ear Training

Research Finding: Teachers who provide computer-assisted instruction to improve ear-training skills help students achieve more than if the students are not given computer-assisted instruction.

Comments: Although instruction related to ear training is routinely given in class settings, often there is not enough class time to give students the drill they need to develop aural acuity. Other forms of out-of-class drill such as self-practice do not achieve as much as computer-based instruction. Computerized instruction functions well in melodic, harmonic, and rhythmic ear training. For instance, children are able to discriminate aurally between same or different directional patterns more easily when a graphic representation of the note pattern is moving on a microcomputer screen than when it appears stationary.

Selection of appropriate computer materials for instruction is crucial since the instructional strategy employed in presenting the material and the organization of the material affect learner attitudes as well as learning. Pacing (the amount of time spent) and branching (provision of alternatives such as skipping unnecessary items) capability of programs help determine their effectiveness for the individual student.

References: Bowman, J. (1984). An investigation of two methods of preparation for college level music theory. *Dissertation Abstracts International, 45,* 779A. (University Microfilms No. 84-13064)

Canelos, J., Murphy, B., Blombach, A., & Heck, W. (1980). Evaluation of three types of instructional strategy for learner acquisition of intervals. *Journal of Research in Music Education, 28,* 243–249.

Hair, H. (1982). Microcomputer tests of aural and visual directional patterns. *Psychology of Music, 10,* no. 2, 26–31.

Hofstetter, F. (1980). Computer-based recognition of perceptual patterns in chord quality dictation exercises. *Journal of Research in Music Education, 28,* 83–91.

Humphries, J. (1980). The effects of computer-assisted aural drill time on achievement in musical interval identification. *Journal of Computer-Based Instruction, 6*(3), 91–98.

Lamb, M., & Bates, R. (1978). Computerized aural training: An interactive system designed to help both teachers and students. *Journal of Computer-Based Instruction, 5*(1–2), 30–37.

Vaughn, A. (1977). A study of the contrast between computer assisted-instruction and the traditional teacher/learner method of instruction in basic musicianship. *Dissertation Abstracts International, 38,* 3357A. (University Microfilms No. 77-25414)

INSTRUCTIONAL STRATEGY

Using Computer-Assisted Instruction: Development of Positive Attitudes

Research Finding: **Teachers can help students develop positive attitudes toward computer-assisted instruction by careful selection of programs to be used and provision of adequate equipment.**

Comments: Computer programs that allow students to progress at their own pace, to branch out when necessary, and to work on needed concepts or skills without pressure from peers are generally perceived positively by the students. They seem to value well-organized instructional strategies with relevant information presented for learning in a logical sequence. Encouragement within the programming sequence is desired by them as one aspect of necessary feedback.

Teachers must explain the intent of each program. In order to meet students' needs, programs must use the full teaching power of the computer. Students are divided as to acceptance of criterion-based instruction, sometimes expressing frustration because of what they perceive are needless exercises being done just to meet designated competencies. When students feel that the program is too time consuming, unenjoyable, and inefficient, they develop an aversion for using it.

Equipment that malfunctions or is not readily available can cause students to react negatively toward a program that might otherwise meet with their approval. The use of headphones may meet with student disapproval. Inadequate work space at the computer may be a distracting influence. The timbre of the sound producer used in the program may cause student complaints.

References: Canelos, J., Murphy, B., Blomback, A., & Heck, W. (1980). Evaluation of three types of instructional strategy for learner acquisition of intervals. *Journal of Research in Music Education, 28,* 243–249.

Fisher, F. (1982). Computer-assisted education: What's not happening? *Journal of Computer-Based Instruction, 9*(1), 19–27.

Greenfield, D., & Codding, P. (1985). Competency-based vs. linear computer instruction of music fundamentals. *Journal of Computer-Based Instruction, 12*(4), 108–110.

Hofstetter, F. (1979). Controlled evaluation of a competency-based approach to teaching aural interval identification. *Journal of Research in Music Education, 27,* 212–213.

Licklider, J. (1962). Preliminary experiments in computer-aided teaching. In J. E. Coulson (Ed.), *Programmed learning and computer-based instruction* (pp. 60–70). New York: Wiley.

Meckley, W. (1985). The development of individualized music learning sequences for non-handicapped, handicapped and gifted learners using the LOGO music version computer language. *Dissertation Abstracts International, 45,* 3573A. (University Microfilms No. 85-03313)

Pembrook, R. (1986). Some implications of students' attitudes toward a computer-based melodic dictation program. *Journal of Research in Music Education, 34,* 121–133.

INSTRUCTIONAL STRATEGY
Teaching Musical Understanding Through Music Videos and Television

Research Finding:	**If music videos and television instruction are to be used in music classes, care must be taken in selecting them.**
Comments:	Music videos shown on Music Television (MTV) and the Black Entertainment Television (BET) channels generally fall into two broad categories: performance (a concert with or without a live audience) or concept (story line or song subject). Because of the popularity of music videos with adolescents, they are sometimes used in music classes for varying reasons. Since television has been found to be a socialization agent, can promote aggressive behavior, adds to stereotypes of men, women and blacks, and influences sexual activity, inappropriate music videos can bring negative influences into the classroom.
	Samples of music videos from MTV showed it to be the domain of the white male, more often aggressive and hostile than helpful and cooperative. Women and blacks rarely appear as the focus of the music videos, but when they do, women are as likely as men to be aggressors. More than half of the behaviors in concept music videos were antisocial. More than half the portrayals of marriage were negative.
	Televised music lessons can function to help students learn other academic skills when structured as a reward for learning. Students show improvement in academic areas and in the process acquire musical knowledge.
References:	Baran, S. (1976a). How TV and film portrayals affect sexual satisfaction in college students. *Journalism Quarterly, 53,* 468–473.
	Baran, S. (1976b). Sex on TV and adolescent sexual self-image. *Journal of Broadcasting, 20*(1), 61–68.
	Brown, J., & Campbell, K. (1986). Race and gender in music videos: The same beat but a different drummer. *Journal of Communication, 36*(1), 94–106.
	Greenberg, B. (1982). Television and role socialization: An overview. In National Institute of Mental Health, *Television and behavior: Ten years of scientific progress and implications for the eighties* (pp. 179–190). Washington, DC: U.S. Government Printing Office.
	Huesmann, L. (1982). Television violence and aggressive behavior. In National Institute of Mental Health, *Television and behavior: Ten years of scientific progress and implications for the eighties* (pp. 126–137). Washington, DC: U.S. Government Printing Office.
	Madsen, C., Dorow, L., Moore, R., & Womble, J. (1976). Effect of music via television as reinforcement for correct mathematics. *Journal of Research in Music Education, 24,* 51–59.

National Institute of Mental Health. (1982). *Television and behavior: Ten years of scientific progress and implications for the eighties* (DHHS Publication No. ADM 82-1195). Washington, DC: U.S. Government Printing Office.

Newcomer, S., & Brown, J. (in press). Influences of television and peers on adolescents' sexual behavior. *Public Health Reports.*

Roberts, E. (1982). Television and sexual learning in childhood. In National Institute of Mental Health, *Television and behavior: Ten years of scientific progress and implications for the eighties* (pp. 209–223). Washington, DC: U.S. Government Printing Office.

Shehan, P. (1979). The effect of the television series *Music Is . . .* on music listening preferences and achievement of elementary general music students. *Contributions to Music Education, 7,* 51–62.

Sims, W. (1985). Television, creative movement and the preschool child. *International Society for Music Education Yearbook, 12,* 103–109.

INSTRUCTIONAL STRATEGY

Using Visual Arts to Reinforce Music Learning

**Research
Finding:** **The development of musical understanding can be enhanced through the use of visual arts.**

Comments: Students' perception of common elements (shape, texture, and color) can be increased through a course devoted to systematic analysis of commonalities. However, students may lack adequate vocabulary to discuss what is perceived.

References: Haack, P. (1970). A study involving the visual arts in the development of music concepts. *Journal of Research in Music Education, 18,* 392–398.

Lawrence, J. (1977). Development of methods and materials for increasing perception of music, visual art, and literature through concepts about elements held in common. *Contributions to Music Education, 5,* 1–88.

Wehner, W. (1966). The relation between six paintings by Paul Klee and selected musical compositions. *Journal of Research in Music Education, 14,* 220–224.

Mainstreaming Students with Handicaps

Research Finding: Teaching strategies that encourage cooperation and interaction must be employed if increased positive interaction between students with and without handicaps is to occur in mainstreamed music classes. Knowledge of special education labels affects performance expectations and may bias evaluations of students with handicaps.

Comments: Positive interactions occur between mainstreamed students with handicaps and other students when instructional strategies include small groups that are encouraged to work together. Large group instruction that does not encourage cooperation does not result in increased positive interactions between students with and without disabilities.

Teachers need to have information regarding students' disabilities to establish appropriate musical expectations and to evaluate them correctly.

References: Cassidy, J. (1987). The effect of "special education" labels on musicians' and nonmusicians' ratings of select choirs. *Journal of the International Association of Music for the Handicapped, 3*(2), 25–40.

Jellison, J., Brooks, B., & Huck, A. (1984). Structuring small groups and music reinforcement to facilitate positive interactions and acceptance of severely handicapped students in the regular music classroom. *Journal of Research in Music Education, 32,* 243–264.

Identifying Specific Instructional Strategies

Research Finding: Effectiveness of specific instructional strategies can be identified and systematically observed in terms of variables describing teacher-student relationships and interactions, lesson content (musical activities and concepts), and lesson format.

Comments: Overt, observable behaviors describing teacher-student relationships have indicated the presence of two instructional strategy styles: lecture style and a guided questions and activities–oriented approach. Appropriate reinforcement techniques and nonverbal communicative gestures have been identified as well. The observation of student behaviors involves such factors as discussion and discovery, self-initiated and teacher-solicited questions and activities, and on-and off-task behaviors. Lesson content and format refers to the relationship between the subject matter covered and the organizational structure of a lesson or rehearsal. The most productive music teachers appear to be those who are flexible in changing their teaching style appropriate to the lesson content.

The control of student on-and off-task behavior through appropriate reinforcement techniques constitutes another overt set of variables describing desirable teaching behavior. Also, the teacher's explicit labeling of that which is to be learned appears to be a contributor to teacher effectiveness.

Teacher behaviors that have positive relationships with achievement include clarity of presentation, focus in lessons, amount of verbal direction time, enthusiasm, and amount of on-task time.

References: Daellenbach, C. (1970). Identification and classification of overt music performance learning behaviors using videotape techniques. *Dissertation Abstracts International, 31,* 4197A. (University Microfilms No. 71-04452)

Dorman, P. (1978). A review of research on observational systems in the analysis of music teaching. *Bulletin of the Council for Research in Music Education, 57,* 35–44.

Froehlich, H. (1981). The use of systematic classroom observation in research on elementary general music teaching. *Bulletin of the Council for Research in Music Education, 66–67,* 15–19.

Froehlich-Rainbow, H. (1984). *Systematische Beobachtung als Methode musikpädagogischer Unterrichtsforschung: Eine Darstellung anhand amerikanischer Materialien* [The method of systematic observation in music education research in the United States]. Mainz: Schott.

Kirkwood, G. (1974). Teacher behavior and pupil achievement in selected elementary music classrooms. *Dissertation Abstracts International, 35,* 239A. (University Microfilms No. 74-14723)

Madsen, C., Greer, R., & Madsen, C., Jr. (Eds.). (1975). *Research in music behavior: Modifying music behavior in the classroom.* New York: Teachers College Press.

Madsen, C., Jr., & Madsen, C. (1983). *Teaching/discipline: A positive approach for educational development.* Raleigh, NC: Contemporary Publishing.

Madsen, C., & Yarbrough, C. (1985). *Competency-based music education.* Raleigh, NC: Contemporary Publishing.

Taebel, D., & Coker, J. (1980). Teaching effectiveness in elementary classroom music: Relationships among competency measures, pupil product measures, and certain attribute variables. *Journal of Research in Music Education, 28,* 250–264.

Junior High General Music Strategies

3

Using Keyboards

Research Finding: Using class piano experiences in the general music classroom can improve the achievement of students.

Comments: Students' music achievement, attitudes toward music, and confidence in music ability improve when participating in class piano. Students experienced in class piano instruction can discriminate meter more accurately than can students having little or no similar background.

Teachers should consider the multiple positive outcomes of using class piano in their curricula.

References: Curt, M. (1971). The use of electronic pianos to facilitate learning in seventh-grade general music classes. *Dissertation Abstracts International, 32,* 997A. (University Microfilms No. 71-13295)

Martinez, H. (1976). The development and investigation of a piano curriculum for improving music reading skills in a general music class. *Dissertation Abstracts International, 36,* 4841A. (University Microfilms No. 76-2671)

Wig, J., & Boyle, J. (1982). The effect of keyboard learning experiences on middle school general music students' music achievement and attitudes. *Journal of Research in Music Education, 30,* 163–172.

INSTRUCTIONAL STRATEGY
Developing Listening Skills

Research Finding: **A number of specific teaching techniques (for example, tracking, use of notation themes and visual representations, programmed instruction, use of positive and negative exemplars of musical styles, and attending concerts) have been found helpful in developing music listening and appreciation skills.**

Comments: To teach recognition of a particular musical style, it is best to use both positive and negative examples of the stylistic concepts rather than just representative examples. For example, in focusing on impressionist harmony, play excerpts of this style and contrast these with exemplars from the Baroque era, that is, a negative example of the style. Examples from the visual arts also help manifest the more abstract aural concepts of music style.

Seventh-grade students who are musically unsophisticated can be taught to keep track of the unfolding forms of unfamiliar minuets or sonata-allegro movements with only minimal initiation to the rudiments of music theory. Sequential step-by-step programs used in programmed instruction can promote musical analysis of recorded works.

Learning modes calling for student participation and ego involvement are more effective than just listening to taped excerpts of musical works, even if the tapes have explanations. Although notated themes may be helpful at the junior high school level, they may be of less value at the elementary school level. Notated examples to accompany listening can be used effectively in the secondary school.

Attendance at symphony concerts, where appropriate commentary is provided, promotes listening skills.

Four approaches to organizing content of music listening courses can be identified: the popular presentation, which begins with familiar music; the associational presentation, which proceeds from the simple to the more complex; the chronological presentation; and the evolutionary presentation, in which musical form is studied in a flexible, evolutionary process from folk song through suite, sonata, and symphony.

Teaching form in recorded music is best approached by beginning with the folk song and then proceeding to more abstract instrumental music.

Emphasis should be placed on teaching musical concepts during the listening lesson, since awareness of these concepts results in more interested and responsive listeners.

References: Duerksen, G. (1968). Recognition of repeated and altered thematic materials in music. *Journal of Research in Music Education, 16,* 3–30.

Getz, R. (1966). The effects of repetition on listening response. *Journal of Research in Music Education, 14,* 178–192.

Graham, J. (1965). The teaching of listening skills through music lessons in fourth and fifth grade classrooms. *Dissertation Abstracts International, 26.* 7114. (University Microfilms No. 66-05987)

Haack, P. (1969). A study in the development of music listening skills of secondary school students. *Journal of Research in Music Education, 17,* 193–201.

Haack, P. (1970). A study involving the visual arts in the development of musical concepts. *Journal of Research in Music Education, 18,* 392–398.

Haack, P. (1972). Use of positive and negative examples in teaching the concept of music style. *Journal of Research in Music Education, 20,* 456–461.

Hair, H. (1987). Children's responses to music stimuli verbal/nonverbal, aural/visual mode. In C. Madsen & C. Prickett (Eds.), *Applications of research in music behavior* (pp. 15–25). Tuscaloosa: University Press of Alabama.

Hare, R. (1959). The pedagogical principles of music appreciation. *Dissertation Abstracts International, 19,* 3320. (University Microfilms No. 59-01682)

Hedden, S. (1980). Development of music listening skills. *Bulletin of the Council for Research in Music Education, 64,* 12–22.

Nelson, G. (1973). A chronometric approach to the study of form in seventh-grade general music classes. *Dissertation Abstracts International, 34,* 811A. (University Microfilms No. 73-18135)

O'Connor, M. (1976). Development of discriminatory music listening skills in the junior high school utilizing programmed instruction. *Dissertation Abstracts International, 37,* 1446A. (University Microfilms No. 76-21332)

Rasmussen, W. (1966). An experiment in developing basic listening skills through programmed instruction. *Dissertation Abstracts International, 26,* 7359A. (University Microfilms No. 66-05492)

Shehan, P. (1986). Music instruction for the live concert performance. *Bulletin of the Council for Research in Music Education, 88,* 51–58.

Sigurdson, G. (1971). The effect of a live symphonic concert experience on listening skills and interests in music. *Dissertation Abstracts International, 32,* 3357A. (University Microfilms No. 71-31304)

Smith, A. (1973). Feasibility of tracing music form as a cognitive listening objective. *Journal of Research in Music Education, 21,* 200–213.

Thompson, K. (1972). Relative effectiveness of aural perception of televised verbal descriptions and visual representations of selected musical events. *Contributions to Music Education, 1,* 68–83.

Zumbrunn, K. (1972). A guided listening program in twentieth-century music for junior high students. *Journal of Research in Music Education, 20,* 370–378.

INSTRUCTIONAL STRATEGY
Teaching Style Concepts

**Research
Finding:** **In teaching style characteristics of a particular period, it is good instructional practice to use some pieces and excerpts both from the period under discussion and from a contrasting era.**

Comments: Students seem to learn concepts more effectively when music examples are compared to and contrasted with other examples. To illustrate, in acquiring the underlying principles of Romantic music, students should hear examples of Baroque music to contrast with those examples of Romantic style. The use of visual arts also furthers the learning of style concepts.

References: Haack, P. (1970). A study involving the visual arts in the development of musical concepts. *Journal of Research in Music Education, 18,* 392–398.

Haack, P. (1972). Use of positive and negative examples in teaching the concept of musical style. *Journal of Research in Music Education, 20,* 456–461.

Hedden, S. (1980). Development of music listening skills. *Bulletin of the Council for Research in Music Education, 64,* 12–22.

INSTRUCTIONAL STRATEGY

Modifying Listening Preferences of Adolescents

Research Finding: General music teachers who want to expand students' listening horizons and influence musical tastes should note two strategies: Repeated listening to music (preferably over an entire semester) seems to have a positive effect on reactions; and students react positively to music that contains certain "liked" elements.

Comments: Peer approval is a powerful factor in students' musical choices, and there is no proof that analytical listening will modify student preferences. To modify this force and to increase the likelihood of students' acceptance and understanding of types of music other than rock, the teacher is advised to use repetition of musical works and music that contain "desired" or "liked" elements. These elements include fast tempo, dynamic variety, repeated conjunct and diatonic melodies, and driving rhythm.

The teacher should use all types of music containing these "liked" elements.

References: Alpert, J. (1980). The effect of disc jockey, peer, and music teacher approval on music selection and preference. *Dissertation Abstracts International, 40,* 5641A. (University Microfilms No. 80-09822)

Bradley, I. (1971). Repetition as a factor in the development of musical preferences. *Journal of Research in Music Education, 19,* 295–298.

Evans, J. (1965). The effect of especially designed music listening experiences on junior high school students' attitudes towards music. *Dissertation Abstracts International, 26,* 6760. (University Microfilms No. 66-01444)

Getz, R. (1966). The effects of repetition on listening response. *Journal of Research in Music Education, 14,* 178–192.

Prince, W. (1972). Some aspects of liking responses of junior high school students for art music. *Contributions to Music Education, 1,* 25–35.

Tanner, F. (1976). The effect of disc jockey approval and peer approval of music on music selection. *Dissertation Abstracts International, 37,* 3492A. (University Microfilms No. 76-27709)

INSTRUCTIONAL STRATEGY

Selecting Music With Qualities for Listening

Research Finding: **Certain qualities influence what children and adolescents prefer in music.**

Comments: In selecting music for students, teachers need to consider qualities such as tempo, performing medium, musical styles, voices or instruments used, and sex and singing style of vocal performers. Certain attributes seem to be associated with negative reactions: high intensity level, dissonance, minor mode, disjunct melody, slow tempi, and tonally vague melody.

Unsophisticated listeners seem to prefer music that is fast, is instrumental, is in the popular music style, is performed by male vocalists, has singers who have low amounts of vocal vibrato, has a variety of loudness levels, has driving rhythm, has melodic repeats, and has conjunct, diatonic melody.

To encourage a positive listener response to jazz and art music, introduce fast instrumental examples first and progress to slow instrumental, fast vocal, and slow vocal examples in that order.

References: Bauman, V. (1960). Teen-age music preferences. *Journal of Research in Music Education, 8,* 75–84.

Boyle, J., Hosterman, G., & Ramsey, D. (1981). Factors influencing music preferences of young people. *Journal of Research in Music Education, 29,* 47–55.

Geringer, J., & Madsen, C. (1987). Pitch and tempo preferences in recorded popular music. In C. Madsen & C. Prickett (Eds.), *Applications of research in music behavior* (pp. 204–212). Tuscaloosa: University of Alabama Press.

Getz, R. (1966). The influence of familiarity through repetition in determining music preference. *Journal of Research in Music Education, 14,* 178–192.

Keston, M., & Pinto, I. (1955). Possible factors influencing musical preferences. *Journal of Genetic Psychology, 86,* 101–113.

LeBlanc, A. (1979). Generic style music preferences of fifth grade students. *Journal of Research in Music Education, 27,* 255–270.

LeBlanc, A. (1981). Effects of style, tempo, and performing medium on children's music preference. *Journal of Research in Music Education, 29,* 143–156.

LeBlanc, A. (1982). An interactive theory of music preference. *Journal of Music Therapy, 19,* 28–45.

LeBlanc, A., & Cote, R. (1983). Effects of tempo and performing medium on children's music preferences. *Journal of Research in Music Education, 31,* 57–66.

LeBlanc, A., & McCrary, J. (1983). Effect of tempo on children's music preference. *Journal of Research in Music Education, 31,* 283–294.

LeBlanc, A., & Sherrill, C. (1986). Effect of vocal vibrato and performer's sex on children's music preference. *Journal of Research in Music Education, 34,* 222–237.

Prince, W. (1972). Some aspects of liking responses of junior high school students for art music. *Contributions to Music Education, 1,* 25–35.

Wapnick, J. (1976). A review of research on attitude and preference. *Bulletin of the Council for Research in Music Education, 48,* 1–20.

INSTRUCTIONAL STRATEGY
Using Popular Music

Research Finding: General music teachers at the junior high level would do well to incorporate the use of rock and popular music in presenting and demonstrating the various elements of music.

Comments: Students from Grade 3 on prefer rock and popular music when given a variety of musical choices. It seems that general music teachers can capitalize on this finding and use quality rock and popular music to teach musical concepts. Teachers should not use this type of music exclusively; rather, they should use it as a "stepping stone" to more complex kinds of music, for example, jazz and rock fusion, ethnic, folk, experimental, and traditional (classical) music.

References: Alpert, J. (1982). The effect of disc jockey, peer, and music teacher approval of music on music selection and preference. *Journal of Research in Music Education, 30,* 173–186.

Bennett, M. (1975). Make the top 40 work for you. *Music Educators Journal, 61*(5), 32–37.

Cutietta, R. (1985). Using rock videos to your advantage. *Music Educators Journal, 71*(6), 47–79.

Greer, R., Dorow, L., & Randall, A. (1974). Music listening preferences of elementary school children. *Journal of Research in Music Education, 21,* 345–354.

Harvey, A. (1984). The role of contemporary popular music in general music classes. *General Music Journal, 39*(1), 50–53.

O'Brien, J. (1982). A plea for pop. *Music Educators Journal, 68*(7), 44, 51–54.

INSTRUCTIONAL STRATEGY

Improving Listening Skills With Visual Guides

Research Finding: **Visuals designed to "look as the music sounds" can provide simplified scores that, when presented on film or videotape, can guide young listeners to a greater awareness of specific elements of music.**

Comments: A variety of abstract and representational visual aids, such as lines showing melodic contour or blocks showing rhythm patterns have been used to direct students' attention to specific parameters of music while they are experiencing music. Such visuals have been found effective, but not necessarily more effective than other means for guiding listening.

References: Brown, A. (1978). Effects of television on student music selection, music skills, and attitudes. *Journal of Research in Music Education, 26,* 445–455.

March, H. (1980). The development and evaluation of an animated film to improve listening skills of junior high school general music students. *Dissertation Abstracts International, 41,* 3937A. (University Microfilms No. 81-06188)

Thompson, K. (1972). Relative effectiveness on aural perception of televised verbal descriptions and visual representations of selected musical events. *Contributions to Music Education, 1,* 68–83.

Enriching Culturally Deprived Students

Research Finding: **Environmental and socioeconomic factors have a great deal to do with the development of listening skills.**

Comments: Teachers must consider students' background when developing lesson plans for general music. Because junior high students from culturally deprived backgrounds do poorly on tests of listening skills when compared to students from middle-class homes, the teacher must modify listening materials to suit the backgrounds of the students. Tests should be tailored to the experiences and background of the students' abilities. Remedial work should be offered when necessary.

References: McDonald, D. (1974). Environment: A factor in conceptual listening skills of elementary school children. *Journal of Research in Music Education, 22,* 205–214.

Standifer, J. (1970). Listening is an equal opportunity art. *Music Educators Journal, 56*(5), 97–99, 155.

Swickard, J. (1971). A comparative study of musical achievement of students in grades four, five, and six. *Dissertation Abstracts International, 32,* 4653A. (University Microfilms No. 72-07082)

4

Secondary General
Music Strategies

INSTRUCTIONAL STRATEGY
Motivating Students

Research Finding: **Providing students with a choice of curriculum content can effect a positive attitude toward the class.**

Incorporating musical contributions of blacks into general music courses in schools with predominantly black populations can improve positively both attitude toward the course and achievement in it.

Comments: When students can select the content they prefer to study, their attitudes toward music improve. Teachers should encourage increased active involvement with materials by offering a variety of ways in which students can sustain interest in the content and allowing them to choose the content, such as reading material, cassette tapes, written exercises, and other instructional booklets. Participative learning promotes better student learning because students are involved in decisions concerning curriculum content.

Teachers can affect the attitudes of minority students in secondary general music by using materials with special relevance for black youth. General music curricula should include objectives and materials that focus on black music, including recorded examples, bibliography, historical background, and musical activities with relevancy. Positive attitudes toward the curriculum and motivation to study (as well as better attendance records) have been past indicators of motivated general music students.

References: Marshall, A. (1977). An analysis of music curricula and its relationship to the self-image of urban black middle-school age children. *Dissertation Abstracts International, 38,* 6594A. (University Microfilms No. 78-04597)

Pearsall, G. (1980). A curriculum for ninth grade general music: Meeting student needs through areas of designated interest (Volumes 1–2). *Dissertation Abstracts International, 41,* 978A. (University Microfilms No. 80-20631)

Whitworth, L. (1977). Determination of attitude change toward high school general music resulting from instruction in curricular units incorporating cultural and historical contributions of blacks. *Dissertation Abstracts International, 38,* 4649A. (University Microfilms No. 77-30412)

INSTRUCTIONAL STRATEGY
Using Keyboards in Secondary General Music

Research Finding: *Performing musical themes at the piano can aid students in recognizing the themes and recalling their titles and composers. Use of electronic keyboards in general music enhances the development of sight-reading skill, meter and mode discrimination, and a positive attitude toward music.*

Comments: Although some keyboard research has involved college (nonmusic) students, the teaching strategy appears to have potential for high school general music students as well. When students are introduced to themes through keyboard performance, they are able to recognize the themes and recall the composition titles and composers with increased accuracy.

Other applications of keyboard strategies have potential in music reading. Rote playing of melodies at the piano as a prelude to music reading helps both pitch reading and rhythmic reading. Students can sharpen discrimination skills in meter and modes through keyboard work as well.

Overall, keyboard experiences positively affect students' attitudes toward music.

References: Campbell, H. (1983). The effect of a thematic-performance method upon recognition and recall of musical themes. *Dissertation Abstracts International, 45,* 780A. (University Microfilms No. 84-13141)

Fincher, B. (1983). The effects of playing the melody by rote during the prestudy procedure upon sight reading skill development of beginning class piano students. *Dissertation Abstracts International, 44,* 3623A. (University Microfilms No. 84-03971)

Wig, J., & Boyle, J. (1982). The effect of keyboard learning experiences on middle school general music students' music achievement and attitudes. *Journal of Research in Music Education, 30,* 163–172.

INSTRUCTIONAL STRATEGY
Approaching Listening Objectively and Subjectively

Research Finding: **Presenting a variety of objective and subjective approaches promotes growth in music appreciation.**

Comments: Students differ in their responses to music. Some students respond better to emotional context or the use of imagery; others respond more to intellectual, formal, and stylistic study of music. Some students remember pieces better if concrete titles can be given to abstract pieces.

Some students respond to music better using activities such as analysis, sequence, discussion, and study of the parts; others respond better using activities such as movement, use of pictures, subjective activities, and creative art imagery. It is unclear whether analytic listening techniques affect students' expressed musical preferences. The understanding of musical elements may have a slight relationship to affective response. A cognitive-analytic approach has been shown to influence preferences of seventh graders for contemporary music, although conflicting evidence shows that analysis techniques, by themselves, are useful in increasing students' preferences for music.

In general, analytic approaches tend to be more effective after a number of repetitions, whereas the use of story content, imagery, and emotional response may be more effective for an initial, single lesson with music. Written material presented to the listener in the form of program notes or guides to listening could accommodate various learning styles of listeners. Teaching music of the Classical style may require more objective analysis than teaching music of the Romantic style, in which more repetition may be needed to achieve similar affective results.

References: Bartlett, D. (1973). Effect of repeated listenings on structural discrimination and affective response. *Journal of Research in Music Education, 21*, 302–317.

Bradley, I. (1972). Effect of student musical preference of a listening program in contemporary music. *Journal of Research in Music Education, 20*, 344–353.

Haack, P. (1969). A study in the development of music listening skills of secondary school students. *Journal of Research in Music Education, 17*, 193–201.

Hufstader, R. (1977). An investigation of a learning sequence of music listening skills. *Journal of Research in Music Education, 25*, 184–196.

Keston, M. (1954). An experimental evaluation of the efficacy of two methods of teaching music appreciation. *Journal of Experimental Education, 22*, 215–226.

McElwain, J. (1954). The effect of spontaneous and analytic listening on the evoked cortical activity in the left and right hemisphere of musicians and non-musicians. *Journal of Music Therapy, 16*, 180–189.

Prince, W. (1974). Effects of guided listening on musical enjoyment of junior high school students. *Journal of Research in Music Education, 22*, 45–51.

INSTRUCTIONAL STRATEGY

Influencing Attitudes About Music and Musicians

Research Finding: **Teachers can influence musical achievement of their students by fostering the idea that effort and practice, rather than innate ability and talent, are causes of success in music.**

Peer approval is an important factor in music listening choices of high school students.

Comments: Students enrolled in music courses in Grades 4 through 12 have various notions as to why some student musicians do well in music and why others do not. The most frequently-cited reason for success in music was ability, followed closely by effort. As the student gets older, there is a greater tendency to attribute success to musical ability rather than to effort. Three implications of this finding are: (1) Many students believe musical ability is more important than effort and practice for success; (2) increase in magnitude of musical ability is seen as the reason for musical success with increasing grade level in school; and (3) teachers may have some control over prevailing attitudes of students about reasons for success in music.

What factors influence listening choices among high school students? Peer approval, modeling, and adult training were shown to be effective influences on music selection for listening. Whether students study music or not, they select music based upon these influences.

References: Asmus, E. (1986). Student beliefs about the causes of success and failure in music: A study of achievement motivation. *Journal of Research in Music Education, 34,* 262–278.

Hughes, C. (1980). The effect of adult and peer modeling and approval on the music selection behavior of high school students. *Dissertation Abstracts International, 41,* 1463A. (University Microfilms No. 80-22118)

INSTRUCTIONAL STRATEGY
Using Learning Styles as Strategies

Research Finding: The relationship between teaching styles and student learning styles may affect student learning. Learning style includes the way in which new material is assimilated—perceptually (through aural, tactile, and visual processes) and conceptually (using divergent or convergent thinking).

Comments: High school students (ages 11–16) can engage in sophisticated thinking. They can use a hypothesis-testing technique for musical concept formation and to manipulate multiple hypotheses simultaneously.

Both secondary students and teachers can identify their learning and teaching styles, which remain consistent regardless of the subject being studied or taught. There is a tendency for more positive student attitudes to occur when students' styles are similar to their teachers' styles. Thus, once identified and matched, teachers can effect positive learning attitudes.

Teachers should understand the relationships between music aptitudes and cognitive styles because cognitive styles influence auditorily initiated mental processes. Therefore, teachers can use cognitive approaches to enhance aural perceptions. Yet the relationships between aptitudes and style are not always positive. Music composition, for example, involves intuitive and rational music abilities. Some of the learning style components involved in composition relate negatively to musical ability components.

Since an aural learning style is critical to perception and discrimination, teachers must examine listening strategies with care. Age is clearly a significant factor in the listening strategies available to young learners. More complex listening tasks can be managed beginning at approximately age 11.

Teachers should examine their own teaching styles using available measurement devices. Those who find themselves using a single style might consider a more varied teaching approach in order to accommodate all learners.

References: Cutietta, R. (1982). The analysis of listening strategies and musical focus of the 11-to 16-year-old learner. *Dissertation Abstracts International, 43,* 3253A. (University Microfilms No. 83-05630)

Dunn, R. (1983). Can students identify their own learning styles? *Educational Leadership, 40*(5), 60–62.

Heitland, K. (1982). Cognitive styles and musical aptitudes: An exploratory study. *Dissertation Abstracts International, 43,* 2534A. (University Microfilms No. 83-01108)

Moore, B. (1986). Music composition and learning style: The relationship between curriculum and learner. *Dissertation Abstracts International, 47,* 2071A. (University Microfilms No. 86-14387)

Identifying Creativity Among Secondary Students

Research Finding: Although the definition and nature of creativity has been somewhat elusive, recent findings identify specific components of musical creativity. Furthermore, a high level of creativity in music appears to be dependent on a firm grounding of musical achievement.

Comments: Music creativity is often defined and measured in terms of musical processes. Three modes of musical creativity are included in this definition: composition, improvisation, and analysis.

Moreover, in attempts to measure and identify creativity in musicians, when concomitant factors were examined, students scoring high in musical achievement (based on the Colwell Music Achievement Tests) tended to score high on those three modes of creativity.

Teachers must provide a firm grounding in the basic skills of aural discrimination, which are important in establishing a basis for creative ability. Furthermore, general music teachers should consider carefully their students' musical achievement level when assigning activities that require creative musical manipulation.

References: Hounchell, R. (1985). A study of creativity and music reading as objectives of music education as contained in statements in the Music Educators Journal from 1914–1970. *Dissertation Abstracts International, 46,* 3643A. (University Microfilms No. 86-02407)

Webster, P. (1979). Relationship between creative behavior in music and selected variables as measured in high school students. *Journal of Research in Music Education, 27,* 227–242.

5

Instrumental Music Strategies

INSTRUCTIONAL STRATEGY
Teaching Rhythm in Instrumental Music

Research Finding: When rhythmic concepts are the focus of instruction, it may be helpful initially to present rhythm concepts in a monotonic rather than a melodic and rhythmic context. Other students may be presented rhythm materials in a *stable* melodic context with alternating rhythm information.

Comments: Teaching rhythm involves simplification of instructional materials for individual learners. How much simplification is required seems to depend on the individual student. For some, any type of melodic information interferes with the processing of rhythm structures. For others, presenting rhythm patterns in a monotonic or melodic and rhythmic context does not affect rhythm processing.

Research in this area also lends support to the theory that musical stimuli evoke various ways of processing. Certain stimuli are processed more readily at one level than at another. Organization of music may consist of multiple interacting hierarchies. Apparent alternations in tempo, duration, and pitch characteristics within pattern, meter, and rhythmic and melodic patterning have been identified as possible organizers of rhythm information. Research further suggests that classification of major performing instruments is a factor affecting the dimensionality of students' rhythm processing. Instrumentalists tend to organize via tempo, pitch, and duration characteristics within a phrase; pianists and vocalists tend to use both phrase patterning and pitch and duration characteristics.

References: Brown, P. (1981). An enquiry into origins and nature of tempo behaviour: Part II. Experimental work. *Psychology of Music, 9*(2), 32–43.

Byo, J. (1988). The effect of barlines in music notation rhythm reading performance. *Contributions to Music Education, 15,* 7–14.

Kuhn, T. (1974). Discrimination of modulated beat tempo by professional musicians. *Journal of Research in Music Education, 22,* 270–277.

Kuhn, T., & Booth, G. (1988). The effect of melodic activity, tempo change, and audible beat on tempo perception of elementary school children. *Journal of Research in Music Education, 36,* 140–155.

Madsen, C. (1979). Modulated beat discrimination among musicians and nonmusicians. *Journal of Research in Music Education, 27,* 57–67.

McMullen, P. (1973). Preference and interest as functions of distributional redundancy in rhythmic sequences. *Journal of Research in Music Education, 22,* 198–204.

Pflederer, M., & Sechrest, L. (1968). Conservation-type responses of children to musical stimuli. *Bulletin of the Council for Research in Music Education, 13,* 19–36.

Sink, P. (1984). Effects of rhythmic and melodic alternations and selected musical experiences on rhythmic processing. *Journal of Research in Music Education, 32,* 177–193.

Teaching Tonal Patterns in Instrumental Music

Research Finding: **Tonal pattern instruction is superior to the note-by-note approach for the development of sight-reading skills and of auditory and visual discrimination skills.**

Comments: Good readers are those who can anticipate the notes intended by the composer. Instrumental method books often present a new note to be learned as an isolated pitch. The note is given a letter name, a fingering or slide position, and, finally, a sound. This instructional sequence encourages the beginning student to concentrate on individual notes. The strategy results in an irregular rendition that is filled with many stops.

When tonal patterns are taught as a single unit in stages that include an aural presentation and an auditory-visual presentation of the pattern rather than the standard "name-fingering-sound" approach, a higher level of musical understanding as well as proficiency on an instrument takes place. Research indicates that this strategy is particularly effective with students of low musical ability.

References: Gordon, E. (1980). *Learning sequence and patterns in music.* Chicago: GIA Publications.

MacKnight, C. (1975). Music reading ability of beginning wind instrumentalists after melodic instruction. *Journal of Research in Music Education, 23,* 23–34.

Petzold, R. (1960). The perception of music symbols in music reading by normal children and children gifted musically. *Journal of Experimental Education, 28,* 271–319.

Petzold, R. (1963). The development of auditory perception of musical sounds by children in the first six grades. *Journal of Research in Music Education, 11,* 21–43.

Developing Individual Practice Procedures

Research Finding: **Model-supportive practice, assignment of specific practice tasks, and student contracts regarding the frequency, duration, and schedule of practice periods can increase the amount of practice time. A self-report process can increase attentiveness during practice.**

Comments: Teachers can improve the effectiveness of their students' practice efforts by using reinforcement, successive approximation, and modeling during the lesson. The amount of practice time and attentiveness during practice can be increased with the use of contracts and self-reporting systems.

Teachers should spend appropriate amounts of lesson time to establish practice procedures for students so that practice time is sufficient and well focused.

References: Anderson, J. (1981). Effects of tape-recorded aural models on sight-reading and performance skills. *Journal of Research in Music Education, 29,* 23–30.

Geringer, J., & Kostka, M. (1984). An analysis of practice room behavior of college music students. *Contributions to Music Education, 11,* 24–27.

Kostka, M. (1984). An investigation of reinforcements, time use, and student attentiveness in piano lessons. *Journal of Research in Music Education, 32,* 113–122.

Madsen, C., & Geringer, J. (1981). The effect of a distraction index on improving practice, attentiveness, and musical performance. *Bulletin of the Council for Research in Music Education, 66–67,* 46–52.

INSTRUCTIONAL STRATEGY
Developing Total Musicianship in Instrumental Rehearsals

Research Finding: **Improvement of instrumental students' capability to perceive and to describe musical elements encountered when listening or performing does not automatically accrue from a performance-oriented course of instruction.**

Comments: The instrumental objective of developing technical and reading skills often falls short of realizing significant outcomes that are expected from the school music experience. Beyond reading and performing music, instrumentalists should gain an understanding of the importance of structure in music and the ability to make value judgments with respect to the music they encounter in school music experiences.

Music teachers who use class time for the sole purpose of refining performance skills may not significantly improve students' listening skills or descriptive capabilities. Teachers should use a portion of rehearsal time to help students perceive changes occurring in the component parts of music and to understand the relationships that exist between melody, rhythm, harmony, and form. Being able to recognize these components aurally and to describe this recognition verbally enhances students' overall musicianship. The knowledgeable performer/listener, by understanding how music communicates, is then prepared to see individual musical lines as they relate to the ensemble as a whole. The performer also has gained some insight as to what the music communicates, and is better prepared to make value judgments about it. Furthermore, there is evidence to suggest that time allocated to the teaching of listening/descriptive skills does not hinder performance skill development or the musical achievement of the group.

References: Culbert, M. (1974). The effects of using a portion of the rehearsal time for developing skills in describing music on the performance level and musical achievement of high school band students. *Dissertation Abstracts International, 35,* 3486–3487A. (University Microfilms No. 74-28259)

Duerksen, G. (1968). Recognition of repeated and altered thematic materials in music. *Journal of Research in Music Education, 16,* 3–30.

Gebhardt, L. (1974). The development and evaluation of an integrated plan of study providing for increased musical perception and skills by students in the junior high school band. *Dissertation Abstracts International, 34,* 4312A. (University Microfilms No. 74-355).

Hoffer, C. (1977). The development of a musicianship test for students in high school performing organizations. *Bulletin of the Council for Research in Music Education, 50,* 37–41.

National Assessment of Educational Progress. (1981). *Music 1971–79: Results from the second national music assessment* (Report No. 10-MU-01). Denver: Education Commission of the States.

Nierman, G. (1985). The differences in descriptive abilities of band, choral, and orchestral students. *Psychology of Music, 13*(2), 124–132.

Parker, R. (1975). A comparative study of two methods of band instruction at the middle school level. *Dissertation Abstracts International, 35,* 5451A. (University Microfilms No. 75-3165)

Rubin, L. (1953). *The effects of musical experience on musical discriminations and musical preferences.* Berkeley: University of California, W1953, 185.

Stewart, J. (1961). Influence of public school music education as revealed by a comparison of forty selected high school music and non-music students. *Dissertation Abstracts International, 22,* 2822. (University Microfilms No. 72-13945)

Warner, R. (1976). A design for comprehensive musicianship in the senior high school band program. *Dissertation Abstracts International, 36,* 5909A. (University Microfilms No. 76-4785)

Woods, D. (1974). The development and evaluation of an independent school music curriculum stressing comprehensive musicianship at each level, preschool through senior high school. *Dissertation Abstracts International, 34,* 5612A. (University Microfilms No. 74-7849)

Zimmerman, W. (1971). Verbal description of aural music stimuli. *Journal of Research in Music Education, 19,* 422–432.

INSTRUCTIONAL STRATEGY

Incorporating Comprehensive Musicianship Into Rehearsals

Research Finding: **Incorporating the systematic teaching of musical elements into junior high and high school rehearsals produces instrumentalists who are more musically literate than those students involved in "traditional" (for example, performance only) rehearsal situations.**

Comments: A growing body of research is indicating that although students may be able to play their instruments competently, this does not necessarily mean that they are musically aware. What is needed for the total music education of instrumentalists is systematic attention to presenting musical concepts. Perhaps one rehearsal a week could be devoted to using band music to demonstrate and highlight concepts of music. Performance ability is not diminished by devoting attention to musical concepts. Further, research has shown that students who are exposed to this type of teaching improve in the areas of tonal memory, melody recognition, pitch recognition, instrument recognition, and auditory-visual discrimination.

References: Culbert, M. (1974). The effects of using a portion of rehearsal time for developing skills in describing music of the performance level and musical achievement of high school band students. *Dissertation Abstracts International, 35,* 3486A. (University Microfilms No. 74-28259)

Garofalo, R. (1976). *Blueprint for band; A guide to teaching comprehensive musicianship through school band performance.* Portland, ME: J. Weston Walch.

Garofalo, R., & Whaley, G. (1979). Comparison of the unit study and traditional approaches for teaching music through school band performance. *Journal of Research in Music Education, 27,* 137–142.

Gebhardt, L. (1974). The development and evaluation of an integrated plan of study providing for increased musical perception and skills by students in the junior high band. *Dissertation Abstracts International, 34,* 4312A. (University Microfilms No. 74-355)

Haack, P. (1982). A study of high school music participants' stylistic preferences and identification abilities in music and the visual arts. *Journal of Research in Music Education, 30,* 213–220.

Marciniak, F. (1974). Investigation of the relationship between music perception and music performance. *Journal of Research in Music Education, 22,* 35–44.

Whitener, W. (1983). Comparison of two approaches to teaching beginning band. *Journal of Research in Music Education, 31,* 5–13.

Modeling Performance Skills in Instrumental Music

Research Finding: **Effective instrumental teachers should rely more heavily on modeling processes than on verbalization to teach suitable performance behaviors.**

Comments: Successful band directors frequently use both live and recorded models to demonstrate desirable performance skills and techniques. This strategy seems to be superior to verbalization alone, that is, talking about the skills or desired sound. Teachers should show how something goes, not just talk about it.

References: Anderson, J. (1981). Effects of tape-recorded aural models on sight-reading and performance skills. *Journal of Research in Music Education, 29,* 23–30.

The Crane Symposium: Toward an understanding of the teaching learning of musical performance. (1988). Potsdam: Crane School of Music, State University of New York.

Fowler, C. (1987). What we know about the teaching and learning of music performance. *Music Educators Journal, 73*(7), 24–32.

Rosenthal, R. (1984). The relative effects of guided model, model only, guide only, and practice only treatments on the accuracy of advanced instrumentalists' musical performance. *Journal of Research in Music Education, 32,* 265–273.

Zurcher, W. (1975). The effect of model-supportive practice on beginning brass instrumentalists. In C. Madsen, R. Greer, & C. Madsen, Jr. (Eds.), *Research in music behavior: Modifying Music behavior in the classroom*, (pp. 131–138). New York: Teachers College Press.

INSTRUCTIONAL STRATEGY
Controlling Intonation Tendencies of Musical Intervals

Research Finding: **The performed direction of musical intervals does affect the direction (sharpness or flatness) of intonation inaccuracy.**

Comments: Although this research finding was supported by the literature, teachers should be aware of some contradictory evidence regarding the directional deviation tendencies. Some research indicated that students who perform ascending patterns tend to exhibit an inclination for sharpness. Other studies showed that melodic intervals were expanded generally when performed in a descending direction and contracted when performed in an ascending direction. Perhaps some of this incongruity may be explained by differences in the musical or isolated content and the intervallic or scalar content of the performances. Some evidence suggested that the age of the performer is not an important factor. Accuracy in performed intonation is an important concern of music educators and warrants further study.

References: Duke, R. (1985). Wind instrumentalists' intonational performance of selected musical intervals. *Journal of Research in Music Education, 33,* 101–111.

Geringer, J. (1978). Intonational performance and perception of ascending scales. *Journal of Research in Music Education, 26,* 32–40.

Geringer, J., & Sogin, D. (1988). An analysis of musicians' intonational adjustments within the duration of selected tones. *Contributions to Music Education, 15,* 1–6.

Madsen, C., & Flowers, P. (1981/1982). The effect of tuning in an attempt to compensate for pitch/quality errors in flute/oboe duets. *Contributions to Music Education, 5,* 2–10.

Mason, J. (1960). Comparison of solo and ensemble performances with reference to Pythagorean, just, and equi-tempered intonations. *Journal of Research in Music Education, 8,* 31–38.

Papich, G., & Rainbow, E. (1974). A pilot study of performance practices of twentieth-century musicians. *Journal of Research in Music Education, 22,* 24–34.

Salzberg, R. (1980). The effects of visual stimulus and instruction on intonation accuracy of string instrumentalists. *Psychology of Music, 8*(2), 42–49.

Selecting Musical Material for Instrumental Teaching

Research Finding: **Children appear to prefer certain musical styles over others. Tempo also has a significant effect on children's musical preferences.**

Comments: In order for young instrumentalists to master requisite musical skills and concepts, it seems important at the early stages of instruction to use musical materials that are preferred by students. If they exhibit an approach response to the instructional materials, they are likely to spend more time on the tasks designed to promote music learning.

Research on children's music preferences shows a stylistic hierarchy that indicates a preference for rock, popular, and band music over jazz and art music. Furthermore, there seems to be a consistent preference for faster tempi; altered versions of musical excerpts seem to be identified more readily if the tempo has been increased rather than decreased.

References: Geringer, J., & Madsen, C. (1984). Pitch and tempo discrimination in recorded orchestral music among musicians and nonmusicians. *Journal of Research in Music Education, 32,* 195–204.

Greer, R., Dorow, L., & Randall, A. (1974). Music listening preferences of elementary school children. *Journal of Research in Music Education, 22,* 284–291.

Huebner, M. (1976). The effect of three listening methods and two tempi on musical attitude of sixth-grade students. *Dissertation Abstracts International, 37,* 3257A. (University Microfilms No. 76-27394)

Kuhn, T. (1981). Instrumentation for the measurement of music attitudes. *Contributions to Music Education, 8,* 2–38.

LeBlanc, A. (1981). Effects of style, tempo, and performing medium on children's music preferences. *Journal of Research in Music Education, 29,* 143–156.

LeBlanc, A., & Cote, R. (1983). Effects of tempo and performing medium on children's music preference. *Journal of Research in Music Education, 31,* 57–66.

Sims, W. (1987). Effect of tempo on music preference of preschool through fourth-grade children. In C. Madsen & C. Prickett (Eds.), *Application of research in music behavior* (pp. 15–25). Tuscaloosa: University of Alabama Press.

Wapnik, J. (1976). A review of research on attitude and preference. *Bulletin of the Council for Research in Music Education, 48,* 1–20.

INSTRUCTIONAL STRATEGY
Selecting Students for Beginning Instrumental Instruction

Research Finding: In considering youngsters for beginning instrumental instruction, music teachers have traditionally been concerned with factors such as size of hands, teeth, lips, physical size, motor coordination, and other physical characteristics. Physical maturation does play an important part in this process; however, two other important factors in the selection of students have long been disregarded: tonal and rhythmic readiness.

Comments: There is no proper chronological age to begin students' instrumental music instruction. In addition to physical maturation, music teachers are advised to look for rhythmic and tonal readiness. Simply stated, this is the student's ability to tap or play basic rhythms on classroom instruments at a steady tempo and the ability to sing a melody or tonal pattern accurately with satisfactory intonation.

References: Cramer, W. (1958). The relation of maturation and other factors of achievement in beginning instrumental music performance at the fourth through eighth grade levels. *Dissertation Abstracts International, 21,* 540. (University Microfilms No. 58-02786)

The Crane Symposium: Toward an understanding of the teaching and learning of musical performance. (1988). Potsdam: Crane School of Music, State University of New York.

Fowler, C. (1987). What we know about the teaching and learning of music performance. *Music Educators Journal, 73*(7), 24–32.

Gordon, E. (1971). Instrumental music. In *The psychology of music teaching* (pp. 120–129). Englewood Cliffs, NJ: Prentice-Hall.

Hicks, C. (1980). Sound before sight: Strategies for teaching music reading. *Music Educators Journal, 66*(8), 53–55, 65, 67.

INSTRUCTIONAL STRATEGY
Using Rehearsal Time Effectively in Instrumental Music

Research Finding: Ensemble directors do not use rehearsal time as well as they could. Video or audio recordings should be used to record the amount of rehearsal time students actually play their instruments.

Comments: Research in a variety of musical teaching situations points to the necessity for directors to be aware that too little time is allotted for student performance and too much time is spent in categories such as getting ready to perform and "teaching," that is, talking by the director. In some circumstances, less than half of class time was spent in student performance. Directors should attempt to increase student performance time and decrease preparation and teaching time.

References: Caldwell, W. (1980). A time analysis of selected musical elements and leadership behaviors of successful high school choral directors. *Dissertation Abstracts International, 41*, 976A. (University Microfilms No. 80-20349)

Fiedler, S. (1982). *A methodological study of three observation techniques—an observation schedule, participant observation, and a structured interview—in two elementary music classrooms.* Unpublished doctoral dissertation, Northwestern University, Evanston, Illinois.

Papke, R. (1972). An investigation of instrumental music directors' rehearsal behavior utilizing an evaluative instrument with implications for broadening perspectives in secondary school instrumental music curricula. *Dissertation Abstracts International, 33*, 1420A. (University Microfilms No. 72-27787)

Spradling, R. (1980). The effect of time out from performance on attentiveness and attitude of university band students. *Dissertation Abstracts International, 41*, 2989A. (University Microfilms No. 81-00653)

Wagner, M., & Strul, E. (1979). Comparisons of beginning versus experienced elementary music educators in the use of teaching time. *Journal of Research in Music Education, 27*, 113–125.

Witt, A. (1986). Use of class time and student attentiveness in secondary instrumental music rehearsals. *Journal of Research in Music Education, 33*, 34–42.

INSTRUCTIONAL STRATEGY
Peer Tutoring in Instrumental Teaching

Research Finding: **Peer tutoring can have positive effects on the performance abilities of tutors and students in beginning band classes.**

Comments: The instrumental music educator teaching beginning wind players is always faced with the problem of teaching a variety of new skills, symbols, and concepts to a relatively large group of students with minimal instructional time. Individualized instruction may help these teachers deal effectively with the problem. One of the ways instruction can be individualized is to use students as tutors.

The reasons why the tutor-student relationship may be beneficial perhaps relate to one or a combination of these factors: modeling, immediate feedback, and individualization of instruction. Whatever the factors responsible for success, the tutored student's performances of tasks, both in terms of posttest performance scores and the number of exercises completed, often showed significant gain. This was especially true in one study where the tutors used approval rather than disapproval techniques (error-correction) when providing feedback concerning music performance. Some studies indicated that the social behavior of the tutored students also improves significantly.

Peer tutoring has had differing effects on tutor performance. In disciplines other than music, significant academic gains were made by tutors. In others, including a study involving beginning band students, tutors did not benefit significantly, but no poorer achievement was found. How were tutors able to maintain equal performance without their own class instruction? It is speculated that counting aloud for the tutored students, patting the foot, and listening intensely may have helped the tutors learn to play better.

References: Alexander, L., & Dorow, L. (1983). Peer tutoring effects on the music performance of tutors and tutees in beginning band classes. *Journal of Research in Music Education, 31,* 33–47.

Allen, V., & Fledman, R. (1973). Learning through tutoring: Low-achieving children as tutors. *Journal of Experimental Education, 42,* 1–5.

Cloward, R. (1967). Studies in tutoring. *Journal of Experimental Education, 36,* 14–25.

Greer, R., & Polirstok, S. (1982). Collateral gains and short-term maintenance in reading and on-task responses by inner-city adolescents as a function of their use of social reinforcement while tutoring. *Journal of Applied Behavior Analysis, 15,* 123–139.

Rust, S., Jr. (1970). The effect of tutoring on the tutor's behavior, academic achievement, and social status. *Dissertation Abstracts International, 30,* 4862A. (University Microfilms No. 70-9469)

INSTRUCTIONAL STRATEGY
Understanding Anxiety in Performance

Research Finding: Anxiety can be motivational and can facilitate performance ability for some musicians.

Comments: Many researchers in music have assumed that anxiety deters musical performance quality. Research on anxiety assessment in psychiatric and psychological literature indicates that training and ability are important factors affecting anxiety.

There is a growing body of research literature in music that indicates that musicians respond to anxiety as do subjects in other disciplines. There seems to be support for the the idea that anxious situations, such as playing before peers, can facilitate musical performance when musicians possess many years of formal training. For musicians with little formal training or ability, increased anxiety seems to deter performance.

References: Appel, S. (1976). Modifying solo performance anxiety in adult pianists. *Journal of Music Therapy, 13,* 2–16.

Fiske, H. (1979). Musical performance evaluation ability: Toward a model of specificity. *Bulletin of the Council for Research in Music Education, 59,* 27–31.

Hamann, D. (1982). An assessment of anxiety in instrumental and vocal performances. *Journal of Research in Music Education, 30,* 77–90.

Leglar, M. (1979). Measurement of indicators of anxiety levels under varying conditions of musical performance. *Dissertation Abstracts International, 39,* 5201A-5202A. (University Microfilms No. 79-06734)

Raynor, J. (1981). Motivational determinants of music-related behavior: Psychological careers of student, teacher, performer, and listener. In *Documentary report of the Ann Arbor Symposium* (pp. 332–351). Reston, VA: Music Educators National Conference.

Spence, D. (1958). A theory of emotionally based drive (d) and its relation to performance in simple learning situations. *American Psychologist, 13,* 131–141.

Wardle, A. (1975). Behavior modification by reciprocal inhibition of instrumental music performance anxiety. In C. Madsen, R. Greer, & C. Madsen, Jr. (Eds.), *Research in music behavior: Modifying music behavior in the classroom* (pp. 191–205). New York: Teachers College Press.

Photograph courtesy of Jack Pringle

6

String and Orchestral Music Strategies

INSTRUCTIONAL STRATEGY

Applying Suzuki Instruction in String Class Settings

Research Finding: **Aspects of the Suzuki method can be successfully used in heterogeneous beginning string classes.**

Comments: Suzuki instructional techniques found to be particularly effective in school string classes include left-hand finger placement markers, a "listen, sing, play" learning sequence, games to maintain student interest, rote memorization of musical material, and delayed introduction of music reading. Teachers will find that these techniques can be used to facilitate kinesthetic skill development and maintain student interest.

References: Brunson, T. (1969). An adaptation of the Suzuki-Kendall violin method for heterogeneous stringed instrument classes. *Dissertation Abstracts International, 30,* 3967A. (University Microfilms No. 70-02683)

Keraus, R. (1973). An achievement study of private and class Suzuki violin instruction. *Dissertation Abstracts International, 34,* 808A. (University Microfilms No. 73-19369)

Wenzel, V. (1970). *Project Super 1966–1968: A progress report.* Unpublished manuscript, Eastman School of Music, Rochester, New York.

INSTRUCTIONAL STRATEGY

Sequencing Bow Stroke Length in Beginning String Instruction

Research Finding: **The use of short bow strokes at the middle of the bow in the early stages of instruction effectively aids the development of fine motor skills.**

Comments: Students who use long, fluid bow strokes in the initial learning stages develop more bowing problems than do those who use short strokes at the middle of the bow. Mid-bow placement also facilitates the early development of spiccato bowing. It is suggested that beginning string students be limited to the use of the middle third of the bow until they are able to play simple quarter-, eighth-, and sixteenth-note bowing patterns.

References: Gillespie, R. (1988). Identification of factors for evaluating upper string instrument spiccato bowing and a comparison of two instructional approaches. *Dialogue in Instrumental Music Education, 12,* 21–33.

Lowe, H. (1973). A study of the tone quality of beginning violin students using the long bow-stroke approach as compared to the short bow-stroke approach. *Dissertation Abstracts International, 34,* 6024A. (University Microfilms No. 74-03473)

Nelson, D. (1980). The conservation of metre in beginning violin students. *Psychology of Music, 8,* no. 1, 25–33.

INSTRUCTIONAL STRATEGY

Using Alternate Instrument Holds in Beginning String Instruction

Research Finding: A transverse guitar-type hold promotes the development of left-hand fingering technique in beginning string students.

Comments: Neither a sitting nor a standing approach produces any significant difference in the amount of muscle tension or intensity of tone quality in beginning double bass students. On the other hand, a transverse guitar-type hold among beginning violin students is more effective than a conventional hold in developing left-hand fingering technique in students below the sixth-grade level. It is recommended that the transverse hold be used to introduce all new fingering patterns in elementary-level string classes.

References: Dennis, A. (1979). The effect of three methods for supporting the double bass on tone quality and intensity. *Dialogue in Instrumental Music Education, 3,* 43–48.

Dennis, A. (1984). The effect of three methods of supporting the double bass on muscle tension. *Journal of Research in Music Education, 32,* 95–102.

Slayman, H. (1965). Problems in teaching and learning the violin: An exploratory study. *Dissertation Abstracts International, 26,* 5477A. (University Microfilms No. 66-00709)

INSTRUCTIONAL STRATEGY

Improving Intonation Accuracy of Beginning String Students

Research Finding: **Corrective verbal feedback can improve the intonation accuracy of beginning string students.**

Comments: Studies related to the topic of beginning string students' intonation have primarily focused on comparisons of various instructional strategies such as first versus third position teaching approaches, pentatonic versus diatonic instructional materials, finger placement markers versus no markers, computer-assisted instruction versus traditional class instruction, corrective verbal feedback versus visual stimulus and tape-recorded feedback, and piano accompaniment versus no accompaniment.

Teachers should be aware that the use of piano accompaniment actually has a negative effect on both intonation and rhythmic consistency, and corrective verbal feedback has the most positive effect on intonation—particularly when specific inaccuracies are identified and corrected as they occur.

References: Cowden, R. (1969). A comparison of the effectiveness of first and third position approaches to violin instruction. *Dissertation Abstracts International, 30,* 3039A. (University Microfilms No. 69-22113)

Eisele, M. (1985). Development and validation of a computer-assisted instructional lesson for teaching intonation discrimination skills to violin and viola students. *Dissertation Abstracts International, 46,* 3642A. (University Microfilms No. 86-03297)

English, W. (1985). The relative effectiveness of the amount of piano accompaniment in beginning strings class instruction. *Dissertation Abstracts International, 46,* 1550A. (University Microfilms No. 85-17698)

Kantorski, V. (1986). String instrument intonation in upper and lower registers: The effects of accompaniment. *Journal of Research in Music Education, 34,* 200–210.

Maag, R. (1974). A comparison of the effectiveness of pentatonic versus diatonic instruction in the intonation of beginning string students. *Dissertation Abstracts International, 35,* 5081A. (University Microfilms No. 75-04302)

Salzberg, R. (1980). The effects of visual stimulus and instruction on intonation accuracy of string instrumentalists. *Psychology of Music, 8,* no. 2, 42–49.

Smith, C. (1985). Effect of finger placement markers on the development of intonation accuracy in beginning string students. *Dialogue in Instrumental Music Education, 9,* 62–70.

Smith, C. (1987). The effect of finger placement markers on the development of intonation accuracy in fourth and fifth-grade beginning string students. *Dialogue in Instrumental Music Education, 11,* 75–81.

Reinforcement and Modeling of Kinesthetic String Skills

Research Finding: **The behavioral techniques of reinforcement and modeling can be used suc--cessfully in beginning string classes to promote the development of kinesthetic performance skills.**

Comments: Two behavioral techniques that have been found to be particularly effective in developing kinesthetic performance skills are reinforcement and modeling. The use of positive reinforcement is more effective than negative corrective feedback in remedying incorrect kinesthetic motions. Modeling can be successfully employed to demonstrate and develop basic performance skills such as fingering, shifting, vibrato, and bowing. Educators should use these strategies with beginning string students to teach the basic movement patterns that are involved in each separate kinesthetic skill.

References: Harner, M. (1975). Principles of learning applied to beginning stringed instrument instruction. *Dissertation Abstracts International, 35,* 6752A. (University Microfilms No. 75-09565)

Jacobs, C. (1969). Investigation of kinesthetics in violin playing. *Journal of Research in Music Education, 17,* 112–114.

Rolland, P. (1971). *Development and trial of a two-year program of string instruction: Final report* (Report No. BR-5-1182). Urbana: University of Illinois, School of Music. (ERIC Document Reproduction Service No. ED 063323)

Salzberg, R., & Salzberg, C. (1981). Praise and corrective feedback in the remediation of incorrect left-hand positions of elementary string players. *Journal of Research in Music Education, 29,* 125–133.

Teaching Meter Patterns to Beginning String Students

Research Finding: **Conceptual understanding of meter patterns can be facilitated in beginning string students through the use of movement to music.**

Comments: Beginning string students pass through several stages in their ability to conceptualize rhythm and meter patterns. Interestingly, their understanding does not always correspond to their performance abilities. Teachers who work with children under the age of 9 can facilitate the development of meter conservation through the use of bowing patterns that employ one bow per beat. More complicated rhythm and meter concepts should be introduced through movement to music.

References: Nelson, D. (1980). The conservation of metre in beginning violin students. *Psychology of Music, 8,* no. 1, 25–33.

Nelson, D. (1984). The conservation of rhythm in Suzuki violin students: A task validation study. *Journal of Research in Music Education, 32,* 25–34.

Serafine, M. (1980). Piagetian research in music. *Bulletin of the Council for Research in Music Education, 62,* 1–21.

Webster, P., & Zimmerman, M. (1983). Conservation of rhythmic and tonal patterns. *Bulletin of the Council for Research in Music Education, 71,* 28–49.

Zimmerman, M., & Sechrest, L. (1986). *How children conceptually organize musical sounds: Final report* (Report No. 5-025). Evanston, IL: Northwestern University, School of Music. (ERIC Document Reproduction Service No. ED 028200)

INSTRUCTIONAL STRATEGY
Teaching Music Reading to Beginning String Students

Research Finding: **Beginning string students master music reading and basic kinesthetic skills at a fairly rapid rate when the two are taught separately in the early stages of instruction.**

Comments: Beginning string students have little difficulty learning to read traditional music notation when it is gradually introduced and after they have acquired basic bowing and fingering skills. This instructional sequence has been studied in the context of beginning instrumental instruction and has been verified with similar findings.

Instructional strategies found to be particularly effective in developing music reading skills include using a form of numerical notation that indicates string and finger number prior to the introduction of traditional notation, asking students to say names of the notes without playing them, and having students sing and silently finger the notes.

Teachers should separate the presentation of kinesthetic skills and music reading skills in the initial stages of string instruction so that students are not required to master more than one complex skill at a time.

References: Gutzmacher, R. (1985). The effect of tonal pattern training on the aural perception, reading recognition and melodic sight-reading achievement of first year instrumental music students. *Dissertation Abstracts International, 46,* 1223A. (University Microfilms No. 85-14172)

Jarvis, W. (1981). The effectiveness of verbalization upon the recognition and performance of instrumental music notation. *Dissertation Abstracts International, 42,* 1528A. (University Microfilms No. 81-20827)

Yarborough, W. (1968). Demonstration and research program for teaching young string students. *Bulletin of the Council for Research in Music Education, 12,* 26–31.

INSTRUCTIONAL STRATEGY

Teaching Basic Musicianship in Beginning String Classes

Research Finding: **An approach to beginning string class instruction that emphasizes basic musicianship effectively promotes the development of both kinesthetic performance skills and conceptual understanding about the structure of music.**

Comments: The concepts of pitch, rhythm, dynamics, timbre, form, and style can be taught through the use of a teaching strategy that emphasizes such activities as performing, analyzing, and composing music. Students who receive information about the elements of music as they learn to play their instruments not only master basic technical skills at a rapid rate, but also acquire an increased awareness of how these elements contribute to the total expressiveness of music. Teachers should provide such conceptual information during beginning string classes to aid the overall development of musicality.

References: Fink, P. (1973). The development and evaluation of instructional materials for a beginning class in heterogeneous strings including guitar. *Dissertation Abstracts International, 34,* 2678A. (University Microfilms No. 73-25907)

Wentworth, C. (1977). A program for teaching musicianship in the first year of class string instruction. *Dissertation Abstracts International, 38,* 7203A. (University Microfilms No. 78-07964)

Choral Music
Education Strategies

7

INSTRUCTIONAL STRATEGY
Developing Choral Rehearsal Objectives

Research Finding: **There is general agreement that certain procedures are desirable and teachable in the rehearsal setting, although methods for achieving these goals vary.**

Comments: In order to establish appropriate course objectives and lesson plans, choral directors must have some idea what outcomes are desired by the profession and which of these are capable of being taught within the choral rehearsal. Music educators charged with the preparation of future generations of teachers must be certain that choral directors are aware of these outcomes, of a variety of ways of reaching the singers, and of which procedures have potential for broad application to singers of disparate backgrounds.

Goals most often seen as appropriate include consistent vowels, accurate pitch, blend, music reading, posture, breathing, relaxation and expressive stylistic elements. The largest impediment for adolescents in achieving these goals is inappropriate rehearsal technique. Acknowledgment of these goals and strategies to achieve them will assist beginning teachers in the development of proper class activities.

References: Decker, W. (1976). A study of vocal pedagogy for the choral rehearsal based on theories presented in published literature from 1960–1970 and on interviews and observations of selected choral directors. *Dissertation Abstracts International, 36,* 7920A. (University Microfilms No. 76-12037)

Garretson, R. (1955). A study to identify specific teaching problems confronting Illinois high school choral directors. *Dissertation Abstracts International,* W1955, 184.

Latherow, R. (1962). An overview of the teaching of vocal music in secondary schools. *Dissertation Abstracts International, 23,* 4379. (University Microfilms No. 63-02266)

McCoy, C. (1986). The effects of movement as a rehearsal technique on performance, meter discrimination ability, and attitude of members of high school choral ensembles. *Dissertation Abstracts International, 47,* 2940A. (University Microfilms 86-28132)

Developing Listening and Analysis Skills Among Choral Directors

Research Finding: The most frequently used method of harmonic study is the piano, with silent study of scores ranking second. Conductors choose literature based primarily upon its harmonic structure, and melody plays a secondary role. There is no difference between preservice and in-service teachers' ability to detect errors while listening to ensemble performance of four-part chords.

Comments: Harmonic aspects of choral work are more influential in music selection, but aural analysis of harmonic structure by conductors does not improve with time. Two possible implications can be seen. Either further consideration needs to be placed upon the training in harmony for prospective choral directors, or further emphasis needs to extend to melodic characteristics in music. It is ineffective for directors, having chosen a work because of its harmonic structure (often displayed at the keyboard), to be unable to correct choirs in performance of the harmonic passages. If, indeed, directors are predisposed to listen in a linear manner to choral performances, training should be afforded in methods of error detection based upon that strategy.

References: Gonzo, C. (1969). An analysis of factors related to choral teachers' ability to detect pitch errors while reading the score. *Dissertation Abstracts International, 31,* 784. (University Microfilms No. 70-03543)

Killian, J. (1985). Operant preference for vocal balance in four-voice chorales. *Journal of Research in Music Education, 33,* 55–67.

Malone, P. (1985). Development and evaluation of an approach to increasing pitch error detection skills in choral music education. *Dissertation Abstracts International, 46,* 3644. (University Microfilms No. 86-02871)

Nicholson, R. (1953). The harmonic preparation of the high school choral conductor. *Dissertation Abstracts International, 13,* 1217. (University Microfilms No. 0006275)

Teaching Choral Style

Research Finding: Programmed tape recordings of music from various style periods can be used to aid students in understanding musical elements, including style. These results are especially well supported in the area of avant-garde works, where such an instructional tape is more effective than are traditional methodologies in choral teaching.

Comments: To sing musically, choirs must have an understanding of the stylistic requirements of various choral performances. This aspect of choral music can be taught easily and individually through the use of tapes. The luxury of allowing students to learn at their own rate is an added benefit.

References: Howard, C. (1969). An experimental study in developing and evaluating musical understandings in a high school choir. *Dissertation Abstracts International, 32,* 1551A. (University Microfilms No. 71-13416)

May, J. (1976). An instructional tape of avant-garde choral idioms with an annotated bibliographical index of published compositions for use in secondary schools. *Dissertation Abstracts International, 37,* 3491A. (University Microfilms No. 76-02843)

Raspberry, J. (1985). A dimensional approach to twentieth century choral literature for the high school director. *Dissertation Abstracts International, 47,* 115. (University Microfilms No. 85-29975)

Establishing a Structure for Choral Music Programs

Research Finding: Curricula for choral music education majors should be based upon relevant objectives taken from skills that conductors use on the job.

Comments: There appear to be three main areas of concern in teaching choral music on the secondary level: rehearsal procedures, choosing literature, and handling discipline. In addition, there is a wide difference in what experts express as necessary for good choral and vocal education preparation and that which actually exists on college campuses. Experts agree, however, on specific skills necessary for teaching choral music: voice training, conducting, arranging, ensemble singing, sight singing, and form analysis. Most teachers cite a need for ability to read from an open score, yet examinations reveal that teachers on the job seldom use the skill.

Determination of relevant skills should provide direction for evaluation and improvement in the instruction of preservice choral teachers. If music education programs are to provide instruction in the areas accepted by members of the profession as important, more emphasis should be placed upon arranging, sight singing, form analysis, and the ability to read from an open score.

References: Couch, D. (1972). A comparison of opinions concerning characteristics college choral repertoires should possess to meet the needs of students preparing to teach high school vocal music. *Dissertation Abstracts International, 33,* 6155A. (University Microfilms No. 73-11872)

Harrison, R. (1963). A program for the preparation of choral directors. *Dissertation Abstracts International, 24,* 322.

Taylor, B. (1980). The relative importance of various competencies needed by choral-general music teachers in elementary and secondary schools as rated by college supervisors, music supervisors and choral-general music teachers. *Dissertation Abstracts International, 41,* 2990A. (University Microfilms No. 81-01952)

Weise, N. (1960). *Effective and efficient high school chorus, orchestra and band rehearsal techniques.* Unpublished Master's thesis, Ohio University, Athens.

INSTRUCTIONAL STRATEGY
Developing Aesthetic Sensitivity Through Choral Singing

Research Finding: Greater levels of musical understanding provide the capability for more aesthetic awareness of musical performance. Although research indicates that a more aesthetic basis for rehearsal may not provide a difference in attitude, discrimination, or performance of familiar musical styles, it may lead to better performance of less familiar works.

Comments: The emphasis upon performance skills that has characterized much American music education in this century has led many teachers to focus on technical mastery of musical elements at the expense of affective understanding of their use. Programmed self-instructional materials centering on these elements and used in combination with traditional performance-based methods lead to more gains in musical knowledge than do approaches that emphasize only performance.

Students' ability to respond in an aesthetic manner to music is often questioned, even when the students are enrolled in music. Strategies such as programmed instruction, which provide students with a knowledge of musical elements outside the context of a performance setting, may aid in developing knowledge and understandings necessary for an aesthetic response. This response, in turn, develops a stronger choral performance.

References: Hedberg, F. (1975). An experimental investigation of two choral rehearsal methods: Their effects upon musical attitude, music discrimination, music achievement and musical performance. *Dissertation Abstracts International, 36,* 7263A. (University Microfilms No. 76-10840)

May, J. (1976). An instructional tape of avant-garde choral idioms with an annotated bibliographical index of published compositions for use in secondary schools. *Dissertation Abstracts International, 37,* 3491A. (University Microfilms No. 76-02843)

Poe, F. (1978). The development of instructional materials for teaching and performing renaissance choral music. *Dissertation Abstracts International, 39,* 5386A. (University Microfilms No. 79-06720)

Ramer, A. (1965). A survey and evaluation of current methods, techniques and content in vocal performing groups in selected secondary schools in Wyoming. *Dissertation Abstracts International, 26,* 7181. (University Microfilms No. 66-05996)

Developing Behavior-Management Skills in Choral Music Education

Research Finding: **Simulation of behavior management strategies allows more efficient functioning than do traditional lecture and discussion methods. Student teaching does not affect classroom management skills or beliefs to the extent once predicted. Student teachers do not necessarily adopt the skills and beliefs of cooperating teachers in these areas. Off-task behavior, nonperformance activity, and lesser degrees of teacher eye contact are all strongly related.**

Comments: Maintaining order in the classroom is a major responsibility of the choral director. Simulations that place the preservice teacher in positions that are likely to be faced by the beginning choral director are helpful in developing the skills necessary to manage a classroom. Simulations should be favored over the traditional lecture format. Students should be encouraged to formulate appropriate responses to classroom situations and determine the effectiveness of their implementation. This effort exerts more influence over the development of these skills than does the traditional student teaching experience. Simulations should stress the preventative nature of maintaining eye contact with all students and concentrating upon rehearsal rather than nonperformance activities.

References: Brand, M. (1977). Effectiveness of simulation techniques in teaching behavior management. *Journal of Research in Music Education, 25,* 131–138.

Brand, M. (1982). Effects of student teaching on the classroom management beliefs and skills of music student teachers. *Journal of Research in Music Education, 30,* 255–265.

McCoy, C. (1985). The ensemble director as effective teacher. *Update: Applications of Research in Music Education, 3*(3), 9–12.

Yarbrough, C. (1975). The effect of magnitude of conductor behavior on performance, attentiveness, and attitude of students in selected mixed choruses. *Journal of Research in Music Education, 23,* 134–146.

Yarbrough, C., & Price, H. (1981). Prediction of performer attentiveness based on rehearsal activity and teacher behavior. *Journal of Research in Music Education, 29,* 209–217.

Linda Rutledge

College Teaching Strategies

8

INSTRUCTIONAL STRATEGY

Using Programmed and Videotaped Instruction in String Methods Courses

Research Finding: **Programmed and videotaped instructional materials can be used effectively in beginning string classes to teach both kinesthetic performance skills and the conceptual aspects of string playing.**

Comments: Recent technological innovations have made possible the development of programmed and videotaped instructional materials to teach the basic aspects of beginning string playing. Teachers may find the use of self-instructional videotapes to be as effective as traditional class instruction in developing basic kinesthetic skills such as bowing and finger technique among adult students. Nomenclature and fingering patterns have also been learned effectively through programmed instructional materials.

Studies in the area of instrumental music education indicate that this type of instruction can be used to teach pitch notation and basic instrument fingerings. Teachers should consider the use of programmed instructional materials as an adjunct to regular class instruction. Such strategies may facilitate more effective use of teacher-student contact time.

References: Burgess, N. (1974). The application of self-instructional multimedia approaches to teaching violin in a college string techniques course. *Dissertation Abstracts International, 35,* 4219A. (University Microfilms No. 74-30064)

Drushler, P. (1972). A study comparing programmed instruction with conventional teaching of instrument fingerings and music pitch notation for beginning students of clarinet, flute, and trumpet in a flexible scheduled curriculum. *Dissertation Abstracts International, 33,* 1185A. (University Microfilms No. 72-22908)

Miller, L. (1974). The efficacy of a programmed music fundamentals text as an adjunct to beginning instrumental music study. *Dissertation Abstracts International, 35,* 3487A. (University Microfilms No. 74-27455)

O'Neal, N. (1968). The development of a concept of string techniques by a programmed course of instruction for the heterogeneous string methods class. *Dissertation Abstracts International, 30,* 1590A. (University Microfilms No. 69–16389)

INSTRUCTIONAL STRATEGY
Teaching Conducting Skills

Research Finding: Conductors need a mastery of basic gestures, knowledge of theory and history, intensive keyboard study, and a broad background in humanities. Conducting patterns and gestures are best learned from a combination of charts and teacher imitation. Use of videotaped feedback is more effective than non-use, whether the feedback is done independently or with an instructor. Once skills are mastered, students refine them more fully when there is a lab ensemble to conduct. Specific and immediate self-assessment of technique is more effective in achievement of conducting skills than are verbal self-reinforcements.

Comments: There are certain skills and abilities common to any form of musical conducting, as well as aspects that serve to separate the various ensemble genres. These common skills can be identified and should form the basis of courses in conducting. Evidence indicates that imitation and comparison lead to development of the requisite skills and that it is difficult to properly evaluate your own conducting and its relation to a given pattern. For this reason, videotaped examples of proper techniques may be compared with taped examples of an individual's conducting to these models. Using this strategy, conductors demonstrated significantly greater gains in conducting ability than did students who were not provided a chance to compare their work to the patterns.

References: DeCarbo, N. (1982). The effects of conducting experience and programmed materials on error-detection scores of college conducting students. *Journal of Research in Music Education, 30,* 187–200.

Ervin, C. (1975). Systematic observation and evaluation of conductor effectiveness. *Dissertation Abstracts International, 36,* 7034A. (University Microfilms No. 76-11761)

Fleming, R. (1977). The effect of guided practice materials used with the videotape recorder in developing choral conducting skills. *Dissertation Abstracts International, 38,* 2637A. (University Microfilms No. 77-24759)

Gonzo, C., & Forsythe, J. (1976). Developing and using videotapes to teach rehearsal techniques and principles. *Journal of Research in Music Education, 24,* 32–41.

Jordan, G. (1980). Videotape supplementary instruction in beginning conducting. *Dissertation Abstracts International, 41,* 580A. (University Microfilms No. 80-17958)

Keller, J. (1979). The effects of videotape feedback on the acquisition of selected basic conducting skills. *Dissertation Abstracts International, 40,* 5355A. (University Microfilms No. 80-09299)

Madsen, C., & Yarbrough, C. (1980). *Competency based music education.* Raleigh, NC: Contemporary Publishing.

Molina, A. (1978). Choral and orchestral conducting: Similarities, differences and interactions. *Dissertation Abstracts International, 39,* 3909A. (University Microfilms No. 78-24862)

Price, H. (1985). A competency-based course in basic conducting techniques: A replication. *Journal of Band Research, 21,* 61–69.

Ray, W. (1976). Pedagogy of undergraduate conducting as conceived by the presidents of the American Choral Directors Association. *Dissertation Abstracts International, 37,* 4688A. (University Microfilms No. 77-04010)

Yarbrough, C. (1978). Competency-based conducting: An exploratory study. In *1978 Proceedings of Symposium on Current Issues in Music Education Symposium XI* (pp. 62–73). Columbus: Ohio State University.

Yarbrough, C. (1987). The relationship of behavioral self-assessment to the achievement of basic conducting skills. *Journal of Research in Music Education, 35,* 180–193.

Yarbrough, C., Wapnick, J., & Kelly, R. (1979). Effect of videotape feedback techniques on performance, verbalization, and attitudes of beginning conductors. *Journal of Research in Music Education, 27,* 103–112.

INSTRUCTIONAL STRATEGY
Using Rehearsal Time Effectively

Research Finding: **Less off-task behavior occurs in rehearsals of college-level instrumental ensembles when the conductor (1) reduces the amount of time devoted to discussing the music and (2) increases the number of positive reinforcements given to students.**

Comments: Students seem to prefer making music rather than listening to conductors talk about it—even if the discussion is intended to improve performance. When conductors interrupt performances to discuss the music, increased off-task behavior occurs. However, when those discussions include generous, positive comments about the students' performance, off-task behavior seems to be reduced.

Ineffective teachers spend too much time giving directions and too little time giving musical information in ensemble rehearsals. This problem, combined with the use of too many specific disapprovals and too few approvals, creates frustration and low motivation for both teachers and students.

References: Price, H. (1983). The effect of conductor academic task presentation, conductor reinforcement, and ensemble practice on performers' musical achievement, attentiveness, and attitude. *Journal of Research in Music Education, 31,* 245–258.

Spradling, R. (1985). The effect of timeout from performance on attentiveness and attitude of university band students. *Journal of Research in Music Education, 32,* 123–137.

Yarbrough, C. (1988). Content and pacing in music teaching. In P. Flowers (Ed.), *Current issues in music education: Vol. 13. Student and teacher competencies: Interacting for success* (pp. 9–28). Columbus: Ohio State University, College of the Arts, School of Music, Music Education Division, 1988.

Yarbrough, C., & Price, H. (1981). Prediction of performer attentiveness based on rehearsal activity and teacher behavior. *Journal of Research in Music Education, 29,* 209–217.

Yarbrough, C., & Price, H. (in press). Sequential patterns of instruction in music. *Journal of Research in Music Education.*

INSTRUCTIONAL STRATEGY
Using Programmed Instruction

Research Finding: **Programmed (self-instructional) materials can provide effective instruction in theory, error detection, and some aspects of music history.**

Comments: Programmed instruction appears to provided an effective way to teach note recognition skills and historical background of selected compositions to nonmajors and melodic and rhythmic error recognition to majors. Programmed materials are not necessarily more effective than traditional methods, and generalizations must be made cautiously.

References: Jumpeter, J. (1985). Personalized system of instruction versus the lecture-demonstration method in a specific area of a college music appreciation course. *Journal of Research in Music Education, 33,* 113–122.

Ramsey, D. (1979). Programmed instruction using band literature to teach pitch and rhythm error detection to music education students. *Journal of Research in Music Education, 27,* 149–162.

Roach, D. (1974). Automated aural-visual music theory instruction for elementary education majors. *Journal of Research in Music Education, 22,* 313–318.

INSTRUCTIONAL STRATEGY
Using Computer-Assisted Instruction in Methods Courses

Research Finding: Computer-assisted instruction (CAI), automated aural-visual techniques, and programmed instructional materials are useful in helping college elementary education students develop basic musicianship, knowledge of music fundamentals, and music listening skills.

Comments: There are several advantages in using CAI:

1. CAI facilitates placing the learning experience at the center of instruction and deemphasizes student competition.

2. CAI saves students considerable time in developing ear-training skills and makes it possible for students to study at a convenient time.

3. CAI offers individual reinforcement and allows students to work at their own pace.

4. With the use of CAI and other automated aural-visual techniques, much can be learned outside of class, permitting greater efficiency and individualization as well as conservation of in-class time for other needed tasks.

As to mastery of concepts and skills, students in basic musicianship classes can improve in ear-training skills using CAI more than they can in traditional classroom instruction.

Programmed instruction materials have been shown to be effective in promoting a student's understanding of basic music concepts, cognitive aspects of music, and music notation during beginning study of music theory. They also effectively teach aural and visual perception of melodic and rhythmic elements.

References: Ashford, T. (1966). The use of programmed instruction to teach fundamental concepts in music theory. *Journal of Research in Music Education, 14,* 171–177.

Barnes, R. (1964). Programmed instruction in music fundamentals for future elementary teachers. *Journal of Research in Music Education, 12,* 187–198.

Bracey, G. (1982). Computers in education: What the research shows. *Electronic Learning, 2*(3), 51–54.

Deihl, N., & Radocy, R. (1969). Computer-assisted instruction: Potential for instrumental music education. *Bulletin of the Council for Research in Music Education, 15,* 1–7.

Liberles, J. (1975). Developing selected musical concepts for the preservice elementary school classroom teacher utilizing programmed instruction. *Dissertation Abstracts International, 36,* 1364A. (University Microfilms No. 75-20937)

McGreer, D. (1984). The research literature in computer-assisted instruction. *Update: Applications of Research in Music Education, 3*(1), 12–15.

Medlin, D. (1972). A critical review and synthesis of doctoral research in the methodology of music teaching. *Dissertation Abstracts International, 33,* 5768A. (University Microfilms No. 73-10001)

Roach, D. (1974). Automated aural-visual music theory instruction for elementary education majors. *Journal of Research in Music Education, 22,* 313–318.

Saul, T. (1976). Three applications of the computer in the education of music teachers. *Dissertation Abstracts International, 37,* 1867A. (University Microfilms No. 76-21655)

Vaughn, A. (1978). A study of the contrast between computer-assisted instruction and the traditional teacher learner method of instruction in basic musicianship. *Dissertation Abstracts International, 38,* 3357A. (University Microfilms No. 77–25414)

INSTRUCTIONAL STRATEGY

Improving Pitch Perception and Intonation Through Computer-Assisted Instruction

Research Finding: CAI may be beneficial for pitch discrimination when added to traditional study on instruments. CAI sharpens perceptual skills in error recognition through drill and practice.

Comments: Although a number of good CAI materials are available to supplement classroom instruction, teachers planning to use CAI for pitch discrimination and other related instruction should take care in the selection of prepared programs and proceed cautiously in developing their own CAI programs. The programs must be properly designed and sufficiently tested to ensure their effectiveness. It is recommended that teachers pilot test the program with a few students, paying close attention to the following criteria: the instructional model, the feedback mode, and the means of systematic evaluation.

Preservice teachers should consider CAI programs part of music curricula and evaluate prospective materials with the above criteria in focus.

References: Brown, A. (1976). The effect of televised cognitive skills instruction in vocal and instrumental music on students' music selection, music skills, and attitudes. *Dissertation Abstracts International, 37,* 5760A. (University Microfilms No. 77-05752)

Codding, P. (1987). The effects of visual versus verbal instruction on beginning students' tuning accuracy. In C. Madsen & C. Prickett (Eds.), *Applications of research in music behavior* (pp. 272–284). Tuscaloosa: University of Alabama Press.

Eisele, J. (1986). Development and validation of a computer-assisted instructional lesson for teaching intonation discrimination skills to violin and viola students. *Dissertation Abstracts International, 46,* 3642A. (University Microfilms No. 86-03297)

Deal, J. (1985). Computer-assisted instruction in pitch and rhythm error detection. *Journal of Research in Music Education, 33,* 159-166.

Humphries, J. (1978). The effects of computer-assisted aural drill time on achievement in musical interval identification. *Dissertation Abstracts International, 39,* 1403A. (University Microfilms No. 78-15235)

Lamb, M., & Bates, R. (1978). Computerized aural training: An interactive system designed to help both teachers and students. *Journal of Computer-Based Instruction, 5,* no. 1, 30–37.

Lemons, R. (1984). The development and trial of micro-computer-assisted techniques to supplement traditional training in musical sightreading. *Dissertation Abstracts International, 45,* 2023A. (University Microfilms No. 84-22622)

Placek, R. (1974). Design and trial of a computer-assisted lesson in rhythm. *Journal of Research in Music Education, 22,* 13–23.

Schwaegler, D. (1984). A computer-based trainer for music conducting: The effects of four feedback modes. *Dissertation Abstracts International, 45,* 2794A. (University Microfilms No. 85-28296)

Vaughn, A. (1978). A study of the contrast between computer-assisted instruction and the traditional teacher/learner method of instruction in basic musicianship. *Dissertation Abstracts International, 38,* 3357A. (University Microfilms No. 77-25414)

INSTRUCTIONAL STRATEGY
Drilling With
Computer Assistance

Research
Finding: **Computer programs designed to provide drill can effectively assist in the development of aural skills.**

Comments: Programs designed to provide drill in interval identification and sight singing can effectively help students develop these skills. The establishment of minimal competency levels results in students spending greater time with the programs to meet the expectations.

References: Hofstetter, F. (1979). Evaluation of a competency-based approach to teaching aural interval identification. *Journal of Research in Music Education, 24,* 201–213.

Kuhn, W., & Alvin, R. (1967). Computer assisted teaching: A new approach to research in music. *Journal of Research in Music Education, 15,* 305–315.

Preparing Computer-Assisted Instruction Materials

Research Finding: **Models have been constructed and tested for the development of effective CAI materials. Specific strategies within the materials ensure effective incorporation of CAI within the instructional program.**

Comments: Most CAI strategies involve drill and testing. Certain strategies such as the use of a touch tablet in melodic dictation training, the use of LOGO Music computer language, the effect of feedback modes in drill, and systematic evaluation within CAI materials have been found to be useful in instructional design.

Music teachers need to acquire a broad information base to use when selecting computer software for instructional purposes or to assist them in the preparation of their own programs.

References: Greenfield, D., & Codding, D. (1985). Competency-based vs. linear computer instruction of music fundamentals. *Journal of Computer-Based Instruction, 12,* no. 4, 108–110.

Hair, H. (1982). Microcomputer tests of aural and visual directional patterns. *Psychology of Music, 10,* no. 2, 26–31.

Kirshbaum, T. (1986). Using a touch tablet as an effective, low-cost device in a melodic dictation CAI game. *Journal of Computer-Based Instruction, 13,* no. 1, 14–16.

Meckley, W. (1985). The development of individualized music learning sequences for non-handicapped, handicapped and gifted learners using the LOGO Music version computer language. *Dissertation Abstracts International, 45,* 3573A. (University Microfilms No. 85-03313)

Schwaegler, D. (1985). A computer-based trainer for music conducting: The effects of four feedback modes. *Dissertation Abstracts International, 45,* 2794A. (University Microfilms No. 84-28296)

Turk, G. (1985). Development of the music listening strategy—TEMPO: Computer assisted instruction in music listening. *Dissertation Abstracts International, 45,* 2436A. (University Microfilms No. 84-24344)

Wood, R., & Clements, P. (1986). Systematic evaluation strategies for computer-based music instruction systems. *Journal of Computer-Based Instruction, 13,* no. 1, 17–24.

INSTRUCTIONAL STRATEGY
Composing in Music Methods

Research Finding: The use of creative compositional techniques inherent in both the Contemporary Music Project for Creativity in Music Education and the Manhattanville Music Curriculum Program, both of which involve creativity, improvisation, and contemporary music techniques, leads to positive results in teaching music fundamentals to elementary education college students.

Comments: A creative method, when compared with a programmed approach, produces better results in keyboard skills and a more positive attitude toward music.

Aleatoric composition techniques result in a slight increase in the musicality of non-music majors. The use of creative composition leads to favorable results in teaching music fundamentals. Composition allows students the flexibility to compose at the level of their individual performance skills. Composition techniques also develop self-confidence in students.

References: Daugherty, E. (1977). The application of Manhattanville Music Curriculum Program strategies in a music class for elementary education majors. *Dissertation Abstracts International, 38,* 5979A. (University Microfilms No. 78-03970)

Dodson, T. (1980). The effects of a creative-comprehensive approach and a performance approach on the acquisition of music fundamentals by college students. *Journal of Research in Music Education, 28,* 103-110.

Drew, E. (1974). An application of the Manhattanville Music Curriculum Program to the preparation in music of elementary school classroom teachers. *Dissertation Abstracts International, 35,* 1540A. (University Microfilms No. 74-20472)

Madachy, F. (1978). A comparison of two methods of teaching fundamentals of music to college elementary education students: Programmed and creative. *Dissertation Abstracts International, 39,* 1404A. (University Microfilms No. 78-15985)

Wollman, W. (1972). The effect of a contemporary compositional process derived from aleatory techniques on the musicality of college level non-music majors. *Dissertation Abstracts International, 33,* 1775A. (University Microfilms No. 72-26644)

INSTRUCTIONAL STRATEGY

Developing Competencies of Secondary General Music Teachers

Research Finding: Some desirable instructional competencies for teaching secondary general music can be identified and described. General music teachers consider aural skills and classroom planning competencies to be among the most important competencies for effecting student learning.

Comments: Competencies for describing musical and teaching behaviors of choral-general teachers in both elementary and secondary choral-general music have been identified by teachers in the profession. Teachers rated these competencies with respect to their importance and use. The following musical behaviors were perceived as both important and frequently used: sight singing, accompanying, analysis of musical form, and arranging or adapting music to student levels and needs.

General, vocal, and instrumental teachers rated the area of aural skills highest. College supervisors ranked skills in using multiple arts materials high, and secondary teachers considered reading from an open vocal score a high priority. Many teachers ranked the importance of recognizing each student by name as a valuable competency.

These findings suggest that teacher training programs should help preservice teachers acquire teaching strategies that are specific to their teaching area and specialization.

References: Taebel, D. (1980). Public school music teachers' perceptions of the effect of certain competencies on pupil learning. *Journal of Research in Music Education, 28,* 185–197.

Taylor, B. (1980). The relative importance of various competencies needed by choral-general music teachers in elementary and secondary schools as rated by college supervisors, music supervisors and choral-general music teachers. *Dissertation Abstracts International, 41,* 2990A. (University Microfilms No. (81–01952)

INSTRUCTIONAL STRATEGY
Teaching Classroom
Teachers Music Methods

Research Finding: Specific approaches to training prospective preschool and elementary classroom teachers in music fundamentals and pedagogy have been found effective. Although there are conflicting reports as to what is the "best" approach, the results indicate that some methods are more appropriate for certain desired outcomes.

Comments: Classroom teachers who have taken music education courses, regardless of the method taught, spend more time on music and teach more aspects of music than teachers who have had no music education courses. Classroom teachers with previous musical experience achieve more (in knowledge and skills) than do those who lack experience.

Certain methods, that is, piano and traditional classroom music experiences, seem to teach music fundamentals better than other methods, especially if fundamentals are combined with music education methods. An "activities" approach (modeled on the actual classroom activities of children) can be at least equally effective as courses taught with the traditional method (lecture-demonstration, sight singing, rhythmic reading, and some piano). Both approaches (traditional and activities similar to teaching children music) result in equal achievement in the rudiments of music. An activities approach, however, results in better skills in group singing and playing the piano and classroom instruments and higher individual scores in musical skills, sight singing, rhythm reading, playing chords, and pitching songs. Teaching fundamentals in a manner that models actual classroom activities may be more effective than traditional approaches because skills in performance are enhanced, as is knowledge of the fundamentals of music. Systematic observation and self-evaluation are effective in developing music competencies and decreasing negative mannerisms.

Piano skills may not be necessary for the development of musical concepts by the classroom teacher, since using the Autoharp, bells, and pitch pipe may also be effective.

Dividing music classes into one semester of rudiments and one of teaching methods may not be as effective as a two-semester sequence using an activities approach modeled after actual classroom music teaching. However, a separate methods course after a fundamentals course is more effective in teaching music methods than is a one-semester course combining fundamentals and methods.

References: Fulbright, H. (1970). A comparison between two methods of teaching music fundamentals to pre-service classroom teachers. *Dissertation Abstracts International, 32,* 999A. (University Microfilms No. 71-19367)

Hudson, L. (1973). A study of the effectiveness of teaching music fundamentals and methods to prospective elementary school classroom teachers using two different approaches within a course. *Dissertation Abstracts International, 34,* 4824A. (University Microfilms No. 74-01595)

Jellison, J., & Wolfe, D. (1987). Verbal training effects on teaching units. In C. Madsen & C. Prickett (Eds.), *Applications of research in music behavior* (pp. 135–148). Tuscaloosa: University of Alabama Press.

Moore, R. (1974). The effect of differential teaching techniques on achievement, attitudes, and teaching skills in elementary music education. *Dissertation Abstracts International, 35,* 5896A. (University Microfilms No. 75-07291)

Moore, R. (1976). The effects of videotaped feedback and self-evaluation forms on teaching skills, musicianship, and creativity of prospective elementary teachers. *Bulletin of the Council for Research in Music Education, 47,* 1–7.

Prickett, C. (1987). The effect of self-monitoring on the rate of a verbal mannerism of song leaders. In C. Madsen & C. Prickett (Eds.), *Applications of research in music behavior* (pp. 125–134). Tuscaloosa: University of Alabama Press.

Slagle, H. (1967). An investigation of the effect of seven methods of instruction on the musical achievement of elementary education majors. *Dissertation Abstracts International, 28,* 5098A. (University Microfilms No. 68-8226)

Zinar, R. (1972). *The relationship between classroom teachers' preparation and performance in teaching music in a selected district in New York.* Unpublished manuscript, York College of the City University of New York.

INSTRUCTIONAL STRATEGY

Grouping by Ability in Methods Courses

Research Finding: **Ability grouping in music courses for prospective elementary teachers has little, if any, effect on attitudes or achievement levels.**

Comments: Homogeneous grouping according to the musical ability of prospective elementary teachers enrolled in music methods classes has no significant impact on achievement levels or on attitudes toward elementary school general music. There is little research evidence to show great potential benefits in ability grouping of prospective classroom teachers at the college level in courses similar to "Elementary Music Methods and Materials" or "Music for Classroom Teachers."

References: McGlothlin, D. (1970). An investigation of the efficacy of ability grouping prospective teachers enrolled in elementary music methods and materials courses. *Dissertation Abstracts International, 31,* 1312A. (University Microfilms No. 70-15621)

Tunks, T. (1973). Attitudes of elementary classroom teachers toward elementary general music: The effects of certain aspects of pre-service training. *Dissertation Abstracts International, 34,* 6030A. (University Microfilms No. 74-06156)

INSTRUCTIONAL STRATEGY
Simulating Teaching and Learning Situations

Research Finding: Videotaped and filmed simulation of classrooms, rehearsals, and applied lessons provides effective materials for the training of music teachers.

Comments: Preservice music teachers given the opportunity to view, analyze, and discuss simulated teaching and learning situations presented on videotape or film feel better prepared and in some cases demonstrate greater skill in dealing with actual teaching experiences.

References: Brand, M. (1977). Effectiveness of simulation techniques in teaching behavior management. *Journal of Research in Music Education, 25,* 131–138.

Diamond, R., & Collins, T. (1967). The use of 8mm loop films to teach the identification of clarinet fingerings, embouchure, and hand positions. *Journal of Research in Music Education, 15,* 2241–228.

Saker, J. (1982). An evaluation of a videotaped simulation training program on the perceived ability of band student teachers to deal with behavior management problems encountered during student teaching. *Dissertation Abstracts International, 43,* 2589A. (University Microfilms No. 82-29972)

Stuart, M. (1977). The use of videotape recordings to increase teacher trainees' error detection skills. *Journal of Research in Music Education, 27,* 14–19.

INSTRUCTIONAL STRATEGY
Observing, Modeling, and Refining Teaching Behaviors

Research Finding: Skills in teaching basic music concepts in the classroom can be improved by having teacher trainees engage in obtaining a theoretical perspective on instructional skills observation, modeling practice (field and peer teaching), and feedback.

Comments: The following activities in teacher training experiences have a positive effect on teaching music and on teaching in general:

1. Readings and discussion aimed at gaining a theoretical perspective on human development, educational psychology, and pedagogy

2. Observing others teach, including both excellent teachers and peer teachers, in simulated and actual teaching situations

3. Providing opportunities to practice specific instructional skills in real classroom situations and in simulated experiences with peers

4. Obtaining specific feedback from competent practitioners

5. Self-monitoring and evaluating performance

Students who receive both observation-discussion and presentation-participation modes of instruction do better than those who receive only one or none of these modes of instruction. Students receiving both modes are satisfied with the techniques and find them to be effective, whereas students receiving only one mode of instruction are less satisfied. The addition of videotaped or filmed teaching incidents to the observation-discussion mode improves the value of the first observational experiences.

Both field and peer teaching experiences enable preservice teachers to develop competencies in teaching music and in their own self-perception regarding their ability to teach music. Field teaching and peer teaching seem to be equally effective environments for developing teaching competencies among prospective teachers.

Although observation skills may improve with training, the observer's perceptions of events may vary from the actual event observed. Music education students attend more to the musical product than the social behavior of students and, in classroom observation, attend more to the teacher than to the actions of the students. Observation training and directed focus of attention improve the accuracy of the observation process.

One strategy for evaluating and refining teaching skills is to combine videotaped observations and classroom visitation for in-service sessions after school hours.

References: Burger, M., & Gorman, E. (1978). Field-based experiences in rhythmic expression. *Music Educators Journal, 64,* no. 9, 61–63.

Duke, R. (1987). Observation of applied music instruction: The perceptions of trained and untrained observers. In C. Madsen & C. Prickett (Eds.), *Applications of research in music behavior* (pp. 115–124). Tuscaloosa: University of Alabama Press.

Duke, R., & Prickett, C. (1987). The effect of differentially focused observation on evaluation of instruction. *Journal of Research in Music Education, 35,* 27–37.

Henderson, C. (1972). The effect of in-service training of music teachers in contingent verbal and nonverbal behavior. *Dissertation Abstracts International, 33,* 4218A. (University Microfilms No. 73-02601)

Holt, D. (1973). An evaluation study of two units of instruction for providing prospective elementary teachers with an orientation to selected aspects of general music teaching and learning. *Dissertation Abstracts International, 34,* 4823A (University Microfilms No. 74-03201)

Madsen, C., & Duke, R. (1985). Observation of approval/disapproval in music: Perception versus actual classroom events. *Journal of Research in Music Education, 33,* 205–214.

Morten, H. (1975). A suggested field-based teacher education program: Construction of modules for music education, their implementation and evaluation. *Dissertation Abstracts International, 36,* 3479A. (University Microfilms No. 75-28914)

Parker, C. (1982). A model with four training components for pre-internship teacher education in music. *Dissertation Abstracts International, 43,* 582A. (University Microfilms No. 82-18259)

Prickett, C. (1987). The effect of self-monitoring on the rate of a verbal mannerism of song leaders. In C. Madsen & C. Prickett (Eds.), *Applications of research in music behavior* (pp. 125–144). Tuscaloosa: University of Alabama Press.

Reifsteck, C. (1980). A comparison of field and peer teaching experiences on the development of music teaching competencies of pre-service elementary classroom teachers. *Dissertation Abstracts International, 41,* 3937A. (University Microfilms No. 81–05793)

Analyzing Behaviors Systematically

Research Finding: The use of a coding system for the observation and identification of specific teaching and musical behaviors can be an effective means for teaching those behaviors.

Comments: Students are frequently given "observation" assignments without being provided with specific things to observe or tools with which to observe them. Several research projects have developed systems for observing and recording specific behaviors. Frequency of questioning, incorporation of student ideas, and use of praise were examples of observed teacher behaviors. The process of making these kinds of specific observations contributes significantly to the learning of the observer.

References: DeNicola, D. (1986). The development of an instructional language assessment instrument based upon the historical perspectives of Quintilian, Erasmus, and Herbart, and its use in analyzing the language behaviors of pre-service elementary and music education majors. *Dissertation Abstracts International, 47,* 2938A. (University Microfilms No. 86-26793)

Hedrick, G. (1976). The development of a verbal analysis system for self-evaluation of preservice music teachers. *Dissertation Abstracts International, 37,* 6334A. (University Microfilms No. 77-08590)

Madsen, C., & Geringer, J. (1983). Attending behavior as a function of in-class activity in university music classes. *Journal of Music Therapy, 20,* 30–38.

Verrastro, R. (1975). Verbal behavior analysis as a supervisory technique with student teachers of music. *Journal of Research in Music Education, 23,* 171–185.

Whitehill, C. (1970). The application of Flander's system of classroom interaction analysis to general classroom music teaching. *Dissertation Abstracts International, 31,* 2428A. (University Microfilms No. 70-22623)

Yarbrough, C., Wapnick, J., & Kelly, R. (1979). Effect of videotape feedback techniques on performance, verbalization, and attitudes of beginning conductors. *Journal of Research in Music Education, 27,* 103–112.

INSTRUCTIONAL STRATEGY
Using Peer Teaching Designs for Preservice Music Educators

Research Finding: Peer teaching or microteaching with appropriate feedback fosters attitudinal and cognitive change in preservice teachers.

Comments: Peer teaching or microteaching provides teachers with the opportunity to master various technical skills used in teaching. Reflection on this teaching via videotaping, group discussion, or training in the use of interaction analysis systems (discrimination training) provides opportunities for teachers to consider why they were successful in meeting the objectives of a particular task and to encourage analysis and inquiry into teaching strategies.

When peers work together to evaluate videotapes of microteaching, evaluations tend to be more positive than, but less reliable than, their instructor's evaluations. Some teachers may find that self-confrontation via videotaping, combined with group discussion and discrimination training, provides the optimum combination of microteaching feedback. However, other teachers may find that checklists are just as valuable as technology for providing appropriate feedback.

References: Cruickshank, D. (1981). Evaluation of reflective teaching outcomes. *Journal of Educational Research, 75,* 26–32.

Furman, C. (1987). Behavior checklists and videotapes versus standard instruction feedback in the development of a music teaching competency. In C. Madsen & C. Prickett (Eds.), *Applications of research in music behavior* (pp. 33–98). Tuscaloosa: University of Alabama Press.

Klinzing, H., & Klinzing, E. (1984, April). *The effects of self-confrontation via TV and of additional training components: Group discussion, discrimination training, and practice in a scaled-down situation on the indirectness of teacher trainees.* Paper presented at the meeting of the American Educational Research Association, New Orleans.

Sims, W. (1985). Effects of peer feedback on pre-service teachers' self-evaluation of videotaped teaching. *Florida Journal of Teacher Education,* 115–124.

Williams, E., & Kennedy, J. (1980, April). *The effects of reflective teaching relative to promoting attitudinal change.* Paper presented at the meeting of the American Educational Research Association, Boston.

Yarbrough, C., Wapnick, J., & Kelly, R. (1979). Effect of videotape feedback techniques on performance, verbalization, and attitude of beginning conductors. *Journal of Research in Music Education, 27,* 103–112.

INSTRUCTIONAL STRATEGY
Presenting Models of Desired Behavior

Research Finding: **Providing actual or videotaped models of desired musical or teaching behaviors can be an effective teaching technique at the college level.**

Comments: Students learn through imitation, even at the college level. Actual demonstrations or videotaped examples of musical performance or teaching can provide effective models that students can imitate.

References: Gonzo, C., & Forsythe, J. (1976). Developing and using videotapes to teach rehearsal techniques and principles. *Journal of Research in Music Education, 24,* 32–41.

Rosenthal, R. (1984). The relative effects of guided model, model only, guide only, and practice only treatments on the accuracy of advanced instrumentalists: Musical performance. *Journal of Research in Music Education, 32,* 265–277.

Stuart, M. (1977). The use of videotape recordings to increase teacher trainees' error detection skills. *Journal of Research in Music Education, 27,* 14–19.

Yarbrough, C., Wapnick, J., & Kelly, R. (1979). Effect of videotape feedback techniques on performance, verbalization, and attitude of beginning conductors. *Journal of Research in Music Education, 27,* 103–112.

Role Playing

Research Finding: **Simulation techniques, in which there is a role playing of a difficult situation that the viewer attempts to analyze and solve, can promote skills in teaching music and behavior management.**

Comments: Videotaping simulations are a valuable teacher-training strategy and can improve teacher competencies in a wide variety of areas such as conducting, rehearsal procedures, and preparing for student teaching.

Those students undergoing behavior management training in music using simulation are more effective in dealing with discipline problems in the classroom than are those students without this training.

References: Brand, M. (1977). Effectiveness of simulation techniques in teaching behavior management. *Journal of Research in Music Education, 25,* 131–138.

Carpenter, T. (1973). *Televised music instruction.* Washington, DC: Music Educators National Conference.

Cruickshank, D. (1968). Simulation. *Theory Into Practice, 7,* 190–193.

Waters, D. (1972). The development of simulated critical teaching situations for use in instrumental music teacher education. *Dissertation Abstracts International, 33,* 5024A. (University Microfilms No. 73-05511)

INSTRUCTIONAL STRATEGY
Using Media in Methods Courses

Research Finding: The use of videotaping techniques and instructional television to increase preservice student skills through illustrating teaching strategies, recording students' behaviors as they teach (microteaching), and learning basic musicianship can assist teachers in mastering both teaching techniques and behavior management skills. Self-evaluations of videotaped microteaching have been found to be more accurate and more positive than evaluations completed without videotaped feedback.

Comments: Videotaping is helpful in relating educational theory to practice. Videotaping is useful for studying student behavior and teacher reaction and reinforcement techniques. Microteaching, taping a short, planned lesson among a small group of students, helps prospective teachers develop their teaching skills. Videotaping with self-evaluation forms may be more effective than are mere oral commentary and feedback.

References: Carpenter, T. (1973). *Televised music instruction.* Washington, DC: Music Educators National Conference.

Erlings, B. (1970). A design for employing instructional television in the first term of college functional piano, developed in a comprehensive musicianship program. *Dissertation Abstracts International, 31,* 5445A. (University Microfilms No. 71–10717)

Fierbaugh, H. (1963). The development and evaluation of a series of sound-films for music teacher training education. *Dissertation Abstracts International, 24,* 4726A. (University Microfilms No. 64-03368)

Kuhn, W. (1968). Microteaching: Holding a monitor up to life. *Music Educators Journal, 55*(4), 48–53.

Madsen, C., & Duke, R. (1978). The effect of teacher training on the ability to recognize need for giving approval for appropriate student behavior. *Bulletin of the Council for Research in Music Education, 91,* 103–109.

McClintock, J. (1976). An instructional package for preservice teachers to teach expressive properties to primary children. *Dissertation Abstracts International, 37,* 857A. (University Microfilms No. 76-17285)

McQueerey, L. (1968). Microrehearsal. *Music Educators Journal, 55*(4), 48–53.

Moore, R. (1976). The effects of videotaped feedback and self-evaluation forms on teaching skills, musicianship, and creativity of prospective elementary teachers. *Bulletin of the Council for Research in Music Education, 47,* 1–7.

Rees, L. (1982). The use of self-paced televised instructional programming in music and its implication for Australian education. *Bulletin of the Council for Research in Music Education, 70,* 12–26.

Sims, W. (1986–87). Comparison of music teaching self-evaluations before and after videotape feedback. *Missouri Journal of Research in Music Education, 5,* no. 4, 7–20.

Stuart, M. (1979). The use of videotape recordings to increase teacher trainees' error detection skills. *Journal of Research in Music Education, 27,* 14–19.

Yarbrough, C., Wapnick, J., & Kelly, R. (1979). Effect of videotape feedback techniques on performance, verbalization, and attitudes of beginning conductors. *Journal of Research in Music Education, 27,* 103–112.

INSTRUCTIONAL STRATEGY:
Influencing Student Teachers' Beliefs and Skill Development

Research Finding: Student teaching, generally considered one of the most significant and consolidating experiences in preservice teacher training, may not influence future teachers' beliefs and skill development to the extent generally assumed by the profession or by student teachers themselves.

Comments: Although there are relatively few studies that deal specifically with student teaching in music, many studies in other teaching areas have focused on changes in student teachers' skills, philosophies, behaviors, and attitudes. The findings of these studies seem contradictory. Many studies show that the student teaching experience and cooperating teachers have a significant effect on student teachers. On the other hand, other studies found little or no relationship in teaching behaviors and attitudes between cooperating teachers and student teachers.

For example, conflicting evidence exists regarding the effect of student teaching on behavioral management beliefs and skills. Recent evidence suggests that the influence exerted by cooperating teachers on student teachers with regard to pupil control may be much less powerful than is ordinarily assumed. This implies that college educators who prepare teachers should not abandon efforts to introduce students to new theoretical frameworks for classroom management; these ideas may have an impact on the way future teachers will teach.

References: Boschee, F., Prescott, D., & Hein, D. (1978). Do cooperating teachers influence the educational philosophy of student teachers? *Journal of Teacher Education, 29*(2), 57–61.

Brand, M. (1979). Measuring behavior management skills of preservice instrumental music teachers. *Dialogue in Instrumental Music Education, 3,* 36–41.

Brand, M. (1982). Effects of student teaching on the classroom management beliefs and skills of music student teachers. *Journal of Research in Music Education, 30,* 255–265.

Brand, M. (1985). Does student teaching make a difference? *Music Educators Journal, 71*(8), 23–25.

Burnsed, V. (1982). Student teachers on their own. *Music Educators Journal, 68*(9), 45–46.

Campbell, L., & Williamson, J. (1978). Inner-city schools get more custodial teachers. *Clearing House, 52,* 140–141.

Friebus, R. (1977). Agents of socialization involved in student teaching. *Journal of Educational Research, 70,* 263–268.

Horowitz, M. (1968). Student teaching experiences and attitudes of student teachers. *Journal of Teacher Education, 79,* 317–324.

Hoy, W. (1967). Organizational socialization: The student teacher and pupil control ideology. *Journal of Educational Research, 61,* 153–155.

Roberts, R., & Blankenship, J. (1970). The relationship between the change in pupil control ideology of student teachers and the perception of the cooperating teacher's pupil control ideology. *Journal of Research in Science Teaching, 7,* 315–320.

Sandgren, D., & Schmidt, L. (1956). Does practice teaching change attitudes toward teaching? *Journal of Educational Research, 49,* 673–680.

Templin, T. (1979). Occupational socialization and the physical education student teacher. *Research Quarterly, 50,* 482–493.

Willower, D., Eidell, T., & Hoy, W. (1967). *The school and pupil control ideology* (The Pennsylvania State Studies No. 24). University Park: The Pennsylvania State University.

INSTRUCTIONAL STRATEGY
Making the Most of Student Teaching

Research Finding: A number of instructional techniques have been shown to improve the student teaching experience and attitudinal skills in music teaching.

Comments: Teacher trainees can be taught to identify situations in which they recognize opportunities to give contingent approval relating to appropriate student behavior, thus providing feedback to the student. Sophomore-level student teaching in music can develop positive, generalized attitudes toward teaching.

The use of observational systems—a set of categories used to describe what occurs in a classroom and designed to provide directly observable traits pertaining to the verbal interaction between students and teachers—has aided preservice and in-service training of teachers of music. Most of the systems used are based on Flanders's system of interaction analysis. Students using interaction analysis and observation techniques are less dogmatic in their thinking, use more indirect verbal behaviors, are more aware of a greater variety of verbal behaviors, and use this variety more in their teaching than do their counterparts who use no planned system of observation in the classroom.

Verbal behavior analysis, in which student teachers are sensitized to their verbal actions, contributes to the students' self-knowledge and tends to enhance the development of humanistic teacher-role percepts. Sensitivity to the verbal behavior of verbal actions can be achieved in relatively few conference sessions. Verbal behavior analysis has significant potential as a technique of supervision with student teachers of music.

References: Dorman, P. (1978). A review of research on observational systems in the analysis of musical teaching. *Bulletin of the Council for Research in Music Education, 57,* 35–44.

Epley, W. (1971). Modifying attitudes toward school music teaching through sophomore level experience in elementary or secondary schools. *Dissertation Abstracts International, 32,* 1379A. (University Microfilms No. 71-23995)

Grashel, J. (1984). Doctoral research in music student teaching: 1962–1971. *Bulletin of the Council for Research in Music Education, 78,* 24–32.

Hedrick, G. (1976). The development of a verbal analysis system for a self-evaluation of preservice music teachers. *Dissertation Abstracts International, 37,* 6334A. (University Microfilms No. 77-08590)

Hicks, C. (1976). The effect of training in interaction analysis on the verbal teaching behaviors and attitudes of prospective school instrumental music education students studying conducting. *Dissertation Abstracts International, 37,* 5671A. (University Microfilms No. 77-05817)

Killian, J. (1981). Effect of instructions and feedback on music teaching skills. *Journal of Music Therapy, 18,* 166–180.

Madsen, C., & Duke, R. (1987). The effect of teacher training on the ability to recognize need for giving approval for appropriate student behavior. *Bulletin of the Council for Research in Music Education, 91,* 103–109.

Madsen, C., & Yarbrough, C. (1980). *Competency-based music education.* Raleigh, NC: Contemporary Publishing.

Moore, R. (1976). Effect of differential teaching techniques on achievement, attitude and teaching skills. *Journal of Research in Music Education, 24,* 129–141.

Rossman, R. (1977). A study of directive and non-directive counseling techniques with music student teachers and their relationship to selected personality factors. *Dissertation Abstracts International, 38,* 4648A. (University Microfilms No. 77-31964)

Verrastro, R. (1973). An experimental investigation of verbal behavior as a supervisory technique with student-teachers of music. *Dissertation Abstracts International, 31,* 2781A. (University Microfilms No. 70-24201)

Verrastro, R. (1975). Verbal behavior analysis as a supervisory technique with student teachers of music. *Journal of Research in Music Education, 23,* 171–185.

Wagner, M., & Strul, E. (1979). Comparisons of beginning versus experienced elementary music teachers in the use of teaching time. *Journal of Research in Music Education, 27,* 113–125.

Whitehill, C. (1970). The application of Flander's system of classroom interaction analysis to general classroom music teaching. *Dissertation Abstracts International, 31,* 2428A. (University Microfilms No. 70-22623)

INSTRUCTIONAL STRATEGY

Selecting Cooperating Teachers

Research Finding: **Since student teachers may be influenced by their cooperating teachers, care should be taken in selecting the cooperating teachers for the internship.**

Comments: Despite conceptual and methodological shortcomings in research, students teachers continue to view their cooperating teachers as having the most significant influence on their student teaching experience. Empirical research has been unable to pinpoint the ways in which working with cooperating teachers affects student teachers. Research is contradictory on whether cooperating teachers have a great influence in shaping attitudes of student teachers.

References: Boschee, F., Prescott, D., & Hein, D. (1978). Do cooperating teachers influence the educational philosophy of student teachers? *Journal of Teacher Education, 29,* 57–61.

Brand, M. (1982). Effects of student teaching on the classroom management beliefs and skills of music student teachers. *Journal of Research in Music Education, 30,* 255–265.

Karmos, A., & Jacko, C. (1977). The role of significant others during the student teaching experience. *Journal of Teacher Education, 28,* 51–55.

Price, R. (1961). The influence of supervising teachers. *Journal of Teacher Education, 12,* 471–475.

Yee, A. (1969). Do cooperating teachers influence the attitudes of student teachers? *Journal of Educational Psychology, 60,* 327–332.

Perception Strategies

9

INSTRUCTIONAL STRATEGY
Establishing Conditions Necessary for Aural Perception

Research Finding: Certain physical conditions are necessary when developing increased discriminatory capabilities. Intensity differences create little change in perception of simple frequencies, but a less intense stimulus allows better discrimination of timbre. Greater intensity provides for better discrimination of loudness or dynamic differences. Spatial differences (left versus right ear) exert more influence on discrimination than do other parameters, far more than do frequencies of the stimuli. Although high-frequency hearing capability is not necessary for discrimination, there is a need for temporal separation; one-half second is often needed to discriminate the order of a series of sounds.

Comments: Teachers concerned with aural discrimination of various properties of musical sounds will certainly be interested in conditions that make that process less difficult. Timbre, for instance, may be best presented at a lessened intensity, whereas students seem to discriminate changes in dynamics more easily at a higher intensity level. Development of discrimination through comparison of two tones may be enhanced by the presentation of a standard tone to one ear and the comparison tone to another. Such comparisons seem to be a valid method of developing discrimination; such tests, when based only upon students' descriptions, may test verbal ability rather than aural discrimination.

References: Bradley, I. (1974). Development of aural and visual perception through creative processes. *Journal of Research in Music Education, 22,* 234–240.

Haack, P. (1975). The influence of loudness on the discrimination of musical sound factors. *Journal of Research in Music Education, 23,* 67–77.

Naatanen, R., Porkka, R., Merisalo, A., & Ahtola, S. (1980). Location vs. frequency of pure tones as a basis of fast discrimination. *Acta Psychologica, 44,* 31–40.

Nelson, D., & Stanton, M. (1982). Frequency discrimination at 1200 Hz. in the presence of high-frequency masking noise. *Journal of the Acoustical Society of America, 71,* 660–664.

Stang, A. (1978). Analysis of musical, verbal and experiential factors in the use of a music perception-description test. *Dissertation Abstracts International, 39,* 7210A. (University Microfilms No. 79-12905)

Warren, R. (1974). Auditory temporal discrimination by trained listeners. *Cognitive Psychology, 6,* 237–256.

INSTRUCTIONAL STRATEGY
Developing Rhythm Perception

Research Finding: Of the various elements of music, perception of temporal relationships develops at a relatively early age. Young children use primarily rhythm cues for recognition. Rhythm factors exert more influence over perception than do melody factors. When presented with tone sequences, listeners generate a set of rules for temporal order that provides a basis for detection of variation. Alterations of rhythm patterns affect perception of similarity and dissimilarity. This rhythm perception improves with age, possibly as a result of formal or vicarious training. It diminishes in the very old. Perception of tempo increase occurs more quickly, but perception of tempo decrease is more accurate. Addition of melody to a musical event affects perception of rhythm.

Comments: Much as in the melodic realm, rhythm perception is dependent upon the establishment of a set of rules, a rhythm schema against which all other rhythmic events are measured. Prior to 8 years of age, rhythm awareness is the most influential factor in music perception. Efforts to strengthen this perception should avoid the use of melody; teachers should also recall that extreme alteration of rhythmic patterns aids in discrimination of similarity and dissimilarity, although such alteration inhibits recognition of previously learned rhythmic patterns.

Additionally, when developing rhythm awareness among young students, teachers must be aware that perception of even rhythmic patterns occurs more quickly than does perception of uneven patterns. Listeners are predisposed to develop schema that can be used for greater rhythm complexity with experience.

Finally, the amount of melodic activity is an influential factor in children's perception of tempo; for example, ornamented melodies are perceived as faster than unornamented versions. Teachers should select melodic content carefully when illustrating rhythm concepts.

References: Cohen, A. (1975). Perception of tone sequences from the Western-European chromatic scale: Tonality, transposition and pitch set. *Dissertation Abstracts International, 37,* 4179B. (University Microfilms No. 75-96646)

Duke, R., Geringer, J., & Madsen, C. (1988). Effect of tempo on pitch perception. *Journal of Research in Music Education, 36,* 108–125.

Funk, J. (1977). Some aspects of the development of music perception. *Dissertation Abstracts International, 38,* 1919B. (University Microfilms No. 77-20301)

Geringer, J., & Madsen, C. (1984). Pitch and tempo discrimination in recorded orchestral music among musicians and nonmusicians. *Journal of Research in Music Education, 32,* 195–204.

Kuhn, T. (1987). The effect of tempo, meter, and melodic complexity on the perception of tempo. In C. Madsen & C. Prickett (Eds.), *Applications of research in music behavior* (pp. 165–174). Tuscaloosa: University of Alabama Press.

Kuhn, T., & Booth, G. (1988). The effect of melodic activity, tempo change, and audible beat on the perception of elementary school students. *Journal of Research in Music Education, 36*, 140–155.

Madsen, C., Duke, R., & Geringer, J. (1986). The effect of speed alterations on tempo note selections. *Journal of Research in Music Education, 34,* 101–110.

Sink, P. (1983). Effects of rhythmic and melodic alternations on rhythmic perception. *Journal of Research in Music Education, 31,* 101–113.

Wang, C. (1984). Effects of some aspects of rhythm on tempo perception. *Journal of Research in Music Education, 32,* 169–176.

Yarbrough, C. (1987). The effect of musical excerpts on tempo. In C. Madsen & C. Prickett (Eds.), *Applications of research in music behavior* (pp. 175–189). Tuscaloosa: University of Alabama Press.

INSTRUCTIONAL STRATEGY
Developing Tonal Perception

Research Finding: **The construct of tonality requires an analysis of interrelationships between sounds. This is made possible by the propensity of the perceptual system to reorganize input. The priority of diatonic structure is normally developed by the age of 4 to 6 years, yet discrimination of tonality seldom emerges before the age of 10.**

Comments: Tonality is normally the last of the perceptual capabilities to develop among children. Although recognition of musical events is possible much earlier, ability to reorganize and analyze aural information pertaining to tonality is not found in most preschool or primary children. When working with students of this age, reinforcement of diatonic structures is appropriate, but discriminatory tasks will not be as useful. For older children, as initial attempts to discriminate tonality are made, strategies other than root identification should be explored; studies indicate that root identification is not as effective as a variety of other methods, including evaluation of scale relationships.

Students with low musical aptitude perceive tonal stimuli in a different manner than do those with high aptitude, and low-aptitude students employ a less analytic process than do high-aptitude students.

References: Alvarez, M. (1980). A comparison of scalar and root harmonic aural perception techniques. *Journal of Research in Music Education, 28,* 229–235.

Bar-Droma, Z. (1975). An exploratory study in music perception. *Dissertation Abstracts International, 36,* 4834. (University Microfilms No. 76-03243)

Creel, W., Boomsliter, P., & Powers, S. (1970). Sensations of tone as perceptual forms. *Psychological Review, 77,* 534–545.

Deutsch, D. (1972). Octave generalization and tune recognition. *Perception & Psychophysics, 11,* 411–412.

Deutsch, D. (1980). Music perception. *Musical Quarterly, 66,* 165–179.

Funk, J. (1977). Some aspects of the development of musical perception. *Dissertation Abstracts International, 38,* 1919B. (University Microfilms No. 77-20301)

Gaede, S., Parsons, O., & Bertera, J. (1978). Hemispheric differences in music perception: Aptitude vs. experience. *Neuropsychologica, 16,* 369–373.

Gates, A., & Bradshaw, J. (1977). Music perception and cerebral asymmetries. *Cortex, 13,* 390–401.

Stoffer, T. (1985). Representation of phrase structure in the perception of music. *Music Perception, 3,* 191–220.

Trehub, S., Cohen, A., Thorpe, L., & Morrongiello, B. (1986). Development of the perception of musical relations: Semitone and diatonic structure. *Journal of Experimental Psychology, 12,* 295–301.

INSTRUCTIONAL STRATEGY
Developing Melodic Perception I

Research Finding: **Melodic perception seems to be a process of comparison of an aural stimulus to a general set of rules or schema, previously adopted. In the process, both lateral hemispheres of the brain are involved interdependently.**

Comments: Although preschool children may be capable of recognizing melodic contour, training creates differential hemisphericity effects that lead ultimately to the capability to relate input to a schema, both melodic and temporal in nature, creating melodic perception. No single set of fixed principles may be sufficient to explain all types of such analyses. Thus seen, tonal sensation is a comparison construct, growing from previously accepted standards in such aspects as intensity, spatial difference, and temporal distance in stimuli.

Musical perception, then, must begin with the adoption of a set of temporal and melodic rules, which form the basis for later interactions; preschool children accept such sets through a variety of experiences with melodies that reinforce these rules. Perception at a later age is strengthened as musical events either duplicate of contradict these accepted pitch relations. Because our perceptual system does reorganize input, initial efforts should be directed at establishing a firm framework for this process.

References:
Boltz, M., & Jones, M. (1986). Does rule recursion make melodies easier to reproduce? If not, what does? *Cognitive Psychology, 18,* 389–431.

Carlsen, J. (1982). Musical expectancy: Some perspectives. *Bulletin of the Council for Research in Music Education, 71,* 4–14.

Cohen, A. (1975). Perception of tone sequences from the Western-European chromatic scale: Tonality, transposition and the pitch set. *Dissertation Abstracts International, 37,* 4179B. (University Microfilms No. 75-96646)

Creel, W., Boomsliter, P., & Powers, S. (1970). Sensations of tone as perceptual forms. *Psychological Review, 77,* 534–545.

Deutsch, D. (1980). Music perception. *Musical Quarterly, 66,* 165–179.

Gaede, S., Parsons, O., & Bertera, J. (1978). Hemispheric differences in music perception: Aptitude vs. experience. *Neuropsychologica, 16,* 369–373.

Handel, S. (1974). Perceiving melodic and rhythmic auditory patterns. *Journal of Experimental Psychology, 103,* 922–933.

Krumhansl, C., & Castellano, M. (1983). Dynamic processes in music perception. *Memory and Cognition, 11,* 325–334.

Long, P. (1977). Relationships between pitch memory in short melodies and selected factors. *Journal of Research in Music Education, 25,* 272–282.

Naatanen, R., Porkka, R., Merisalo, A., & Ahtola, S. (1980). Location vs. frequency of pure tones as a basis of fast discrimination. *Acta Psychologica, 44,* 31–40.

Peretz, I. (1985). Les differences hemisphèriques dans la perception des stimuli musicaux chez le sujet normal: I. Les sons isolés. [Hemispheric differences in musical stimuli with normal subjects: I. Isolated sounds.] *L'Année Psychologique, 85,* 429–440.

Sidtis, J. (1980). On the nature of the cortical function underlying right hemisphere auditory perception. *Neuropsychologica, 18,* 321–330.

Stoffer, T. (1985). Representation of phrase structure in the perception of music. *Music Perception, 3,* 191–220.

Taylor, J. (1976). Perception of tonality in short melodies. *Journal of Research in Music Education, 24,* 197–208.

Trehub, S., Cohen, A., Thorpe, L., & Morrongiello, B. (1986). Development of the perception of musical relations: Semitone and diatonic structure. *Journal of Experimental Psychology, 12,* 295–301.

Warren, R. (1974). Auditory temporal discrimination by trained listeners. *Cognitive Psychology, 6,* 237–256.

INSTRUCTIONAL STRATEGY
Developing Melodic Perception II

Research Finding: Perception improves with training. It is the function of both the musical event and the perceiver. Maturation as well as the emergence of certain musical traits allows for the development of greater perceptual ability. Perceptual ability seems to be determined by age, aptitude, and experience. Perception, according to Carlsen (1982), is "the extraction of information contained in the structure of the stimulus." Other studies indicate that training permits the adoption of various techniques for processing the extracted information. These new techniques may include the reorganization of input, which allows an analysis based upon previously adopted patterns.

Comments: Prior to 8 years of age, perception of melodic structure is limited to an awareness of melodic "shape," even though infants and young children can discriminate a semitone in a melodic context. Although priority of diatonic structure emerges by age 4 to 6, the ability to analyze that structure and to contrast it with independent musical events develops at a later age. Teachers wishing to enhance their students' melodic perceptual abilities should choose examples that are diatonic, and when comparing melodic lines, they should ascertain that the general shape of the examples is dissimilar. Subtle melodic differences may not assist young children in making perceptual choices. Specific traits that are highly correlated with melodic perception include higher level singing ability, melodic characteristics, music aptitude, academic achievement, ensemble experience, and theory instruction. These traits should be considered by teachers when grouping students to work on developing melodic perception.

References: Carlsen, J. (1982). Musical expectancy: Some perspectives. *Bulletin of the Council for Research in Music Education, 71,* 4–14.

Funk, J. (1977). Some aspects of the development of musical perception. *Dissertation Abstracts International, 38,* 1919B. (University Microfilms No. 77-20301)

Gates, A., & Bradshaw, J. (1977). The role of the cerebral hemispheres in music. *Brain and Language, 4,* 403–431.

Marciniak, F. (1974). Investigation of the relationships between music perception and music performance. *Journal of Research in Music Education, 22,* 35–44.

Madsen, C., Edmonson, F., & Madsen, C. (1969). Modulated frequency discrimination in relationship to age and musical training. *Journal of the Acoustical Society of America, 46,* 1468–1472.

Pembrook, R. (1987). The effect of vocalization on melodic memory conservation. *Journal of Research in Music Education, 35,* 155–169.

Trehub, S., Cohen, A., Thorpe, L., & Morrongiello, B. (1986). Development of the perception of musical relations: Semitone and diatonic structure. *Journal of Experimental Psychology, 12,* 295–301.

INSTRUCTIONAL STRATEGY
Developing Aural Recognition Skills

Research Finding: Recognition, which has been identified as a somewhat more diffuse, lower level perceptual process, is believed to precede discrimination. It is developed at an earlier age than is the analytic ability that forms the basis of discrimination. Aural recognition improves with age and then diminishes in old age. Very young children use mainly visual cues for recognition, pointing to the primary nature of this facet of music, although rhythm factors continue throughout life to play a larger part in aural perception than do melody factors. Recognition allows a quick, multidimensional comparison of stimuli across a broad range.

Comments: Development of aural recognition skills among very young children should begin with comparisons of pairs of rhythmic patterns that are either identical or extensively altered. Rather than using short rhythmic or melodic segments, which may lead to an attempt at analysis through discrimination of differences, recognition can best be developed through the use of longer examples in which the basic contour or outline of each example is compared with a set of possible matches. The musical schema that may form the basis for perception begins with recognition; when an event contradicts the relations or patterns established within the schema, recognition is hindered.

References: Boltz, M., & Jones, M. (1986). Does rule recursion make melodies easier to reproduce? If not, what does? *Cognitive Psychology, 18,* 389–431.

Funk, J. (1977). Some aspects of the development of musical perception. *Dissertation Abstracts International, 38,* 1919B. (University Microfilms No. 77-20301)

Hartmann, W., Rakerd, B., & Packard, T. (1985). On measuring the frequency-difference limen for short tones. *Perception & Psychophysics, 38,* 199–207.

Gaede, S., Parsons, O., & Bertera, J. (1978). Hemispheric differences in music perception: Aptitude vs. experience. *Neuropsychologica, 16,* 369–373.

Gates, A., & Bradshaw, J. (1977). The role of cerebral hemispheres in music. *Brain and Language, 4,* 403–431.

Krumhansl, C., & Castellano, M. (1983). Dynamic processes in music perception. *Memory & Cognition, 11,* 325–334.

Sidtis, J. (1980). On the nature of cortical function underlying right hemisphere auditory perception. *Neuropsychologica, 18,* 321–330.

INSTRUCTIONAL STRATEGY
Developing Aural Discrimination

Research Finding: Discrimination appears to be primarily a left- hemisphere function in situations where a single aspect of sound is being processed; the right hemisphere is somewhat more specialized for analysis of more holistic, steady-state information. The perceptual process begins with a general recognition and proceeds to a more specific discrimination. Any severe alteration of the stimuli that highlights the differences in stimuli brings about better discrimination. In consideration of a pair of musical tones, discrimination improves if the duration of either tone is increased. Analysis of brainwave responses has isolated a specific beginning and ending of the decision-making process that is the basis of discrimination. Accuracy of recall of verbal stimuli increases with the addition of melody (song) input.

Comments: Teachers wishing to develop aural discrimination among children should remember that recognition ability seems to precede discrimination. Once students are able to recognize familiar stimuli, discrimination of these familiar stimuli and extensively altered stimuli will help students develop the decision-making process. Gradually, more subtle differences in the stimuli can be introduced. Teachers should also remember that discrimination tasks, as opposed to activities such as pitch matching, force a comparison along a single perceptual dimension. Confounding factors introduced into the stimuli seem to cause a lessened discriminatory ability.

References: Funk, J. (1977). Some aspects of the development of musical perception. *Dissertation Abstracts International, 38,* 1919B. (University Microfilms No. 77-20301)

Fyk, J. (1987). Duration of tones required for satisfactory precision of pitch matching. *Bulletin of the Council for Research in Music Education, 91,* 38–44.

Jellison, J. (1976). Accuracy of temporal order recall of verbal and song digit spans presented to right and left ears. *Journal of Music Therapy, 13,* 114–129.

Hartmann, W., Rakerd, B., & Packard, T. (1985). On measuring the frequency-difference limen for short tones. *Perception & Psychophysics, 38,* 199–207.

Lindholm, E., & Koriath, J. (1985). Analysis of multiple event related potential components in a tone discrimination task. *International Journal of Psychophysiology, 3,* 121–129.

Peretz, I. (1985). Les differences hemisphèriques dans la perception des stimuli musicaux chez le sujet normal: I. Les sons isolés. [Hemispheric differences in musical stimuli with normal subjects: I. Isolated sounds.] *L'Année Psychologique, 85,* 429–440.

Sidtis, J. (1980). On the nature of the cortical function underlying right hemisphere auditory perception. *Neuropsychologica, 18,* 321–330.

Music Educators National Conference offers many valuable publications for sale. The following are the MENC "best sellers."

"America Takes Note" Songbook
Beyond the Classroom: Informing Others
The Complete String Guide: Standards, Programs, Purchase, and Maintenance
Guidelines for Performance of School Music Groups
Music in the High School: Current Aproaches to Secondary General Music Instruction
Music Facilities: Building, Equipping, and Renovating
Music Teacher Education: Partnership and Process
Promoting School Music: A Practice Guide
Pronounciation Guide for Choral Literature
Readings in General Music
The School Music Program: Description and Standards
Testimony to Music
Words of Note—Music in Today's Schools: Rationale and Commentary
TIPS: Discipline in the Music Classroom
TIPS: Getting Started with Elementary School Music
TIPS: Music In Our Schools Month
TIPS: Public Relations
TIPS: Retirement
TIPS: Teaching Music to Special Learners

To order or for more information, contact Music Educators National Conference, 1902 Association Drive, Reston, Virginia 22091, 703-860-4000.